Thomas Laurie

Woman and the Gospel in Persia

Thomas Laurie

Woman and the Gospel in Persia

ISBN/EAN: 9783743316607

Manufactured in Europe, USA, Canada, Australia, Japa

Cover: Foto ©ninafisch / pixelio.de

Manufactured and distributed by brebook publishing software (www.brebook.com)

Thomas Laurie

Woman and the Gospel in Persia

MISSIONARY ANNALS.
(*A SERIES.*)

WOMAN AND THE GOSPEL

IN PERSIA.

BY

REV. THOMAS LAURIE, D. D.

CHICAGO:
WOMAN'S PRESBYTERIAN BOARD OF MISSIONS OF THE NORTHWEST,
Room 48, McCormick Block.

COPYRIGHT, 1887, BY THE
WOMAN'S PRESBYTERIAN BOARD OF MISSIONS
OF THE NORTHWEST.

CONTENTS.

CHAPTER I. INTRODUCTORY.
" II. THE NESTORIANS.
" III. THE BEGINNINGS.
" IV. THE SEMINARY.
" V. EARLY LABORS FOR WOMEN.
" VI. REVIVALS.
" VII. FIRST FRUITS.
" VIII. DARK DAYS.
" IX. PRAYERFULNESS OF NESTORIAN CONVERTS.
" X. THE MOUNTAIN NESTORIANS.
" XI. CONCLUSION.

NOTE.

THIS book is an abridgment of "Woman and her Savior in Persia," by Rev. Thomas Laurie, D. D., and has been generously prepared by him and presented to the Woman's Presbyterian Board of Missions of the Northwest, for this series.

Necessarily much of the larger work has been omitted, and it is hoped that the perusal of these pages will induce many to read the original work (303 pages, Congregational Publishing Society, Boston, Mass., price $1.25). That volume contains, among other things, the best map yet prepared of the Nestorian country, a number of illustrations, prepared by a missionary, among them views of the Seminary where Miss Fiske taught, many interesting letters from Nestorian women and several compositions by the pupils, (pages 242-262), one of them the Bible story of Hannah, from an Oriental stand-point, together with many details of missionary history for which this pamphlet has not room. That same want of room has led the writer to try to strike out every superfluous word from these pages.

W. P. B. M. OF THE N. W.

Woman and the Gospel

IN PERSIA.

CHAPTER I.

INTRODUCTORY.

MAY 1, 1816, in the quiet hill town of Shelburne, Mass., Fidelia Fiske began her earthly life. July 12, 1831, she became a member of the church there. In 1842, she graduated at Mt. Holyoke Seminary, and had just begun her work as teacher in that institution, when she sailed for Persia, March 1, 1843. For fifteen years she was principal of the Girls' Seminary at Oroomiah, and of more than a thousand missionaries whom he had known, Dr. Anderson said that none left a brighter record than hers. He adds, "It seemed as though she spoke and acted just as I would have expected the Saviour to speak and act in the same situation."

A returned missionary felt that some written record should be made of her labors, and as he could not induce her to make it, made it himself from materials furnished by her. It was reward enough to have her write to a friend. "I feel that God sent him to do it." It was done none too soon for on July 26, of the following year, she entered into rest.

CHAPTER II.

THE NESTORIANS.*

THIS people are Syrians. They speak a modern dialect of the Ancient Syriac which is the language our Saviour spoke when on earth, and ecclesiastically belong to the ancient Syrian Church. The Patriarch always bears the name of Mar Shimon (Lord Simon) as the successor of Simon Peter. Their country commences on the banks of the river Tigris, occupies the western slopes of central Kurdistan and reaches down to the Eastern declivities to the lake of Oroomiah. For centuries they have been oppressed by the Moslems. They have not been allowed to be merchants, only the coarsest kinds of handicraft have been open to them, and a decent garment has been safe on a Nestorian only when hidden under rags. Mohammedan law gave the property of the family to any member of it that became a Moslem, so when Moslem noblemen seized Nestorian girls for their harems, they claimed the entire possession of the outraged family in the name of their victim at the same time. Their language had no word for home. Several generations eat, slept and did all household work in a single room. This was lighted by a hole in the earthen roof that served for chimney, so that the interior glistened with smoke as though coated with black varnish. The earthen floor was partly covered with coarse straw mats, and in dry weather the earth sifted down from the ceiling of

---

*There is no country of Nestoria as some speak of it. The name Nestorians is ecclesiastical, not geographical, derived from Nestorius the Patriarch of Constantinople in A D. 428.

rough sticks, or, after rain, poured down in the form of mud. In the mountains some houses are half under ground, and occupied by herds and flocks as well as men, so as to utilize the animal heat, for wood is scarce, and dried manure is often the only fuel. The influence of such abodes on neatness and morality need not be told. Yonan wrote in 1858, "Widow Hatoon tries to have family prayer, but it is very difficult. To use her own words, 'we are all in one room and our beds are very near each other. When we retire, as there is no separate chamber, I gather them behind a quilt and talk and pray with them'." Truly where there is a will there is also a way, but how many would follow Hatoon's example? Vermin of all kinds abound. Mrs. Grant burst into tears the first time she detected a certain insect on her clothing, but it was not the last one, for contact with the natives renews the supply, however thoroughly the pests may have been destroyed. Did not the Master suffer in the same way in His seeking for that which was lost? If such houses are full of discomfort in health, what are they in sickness? Mothers often have no better sickroom than Mary found in Bethlehem. Many are born and many mothers die every year among the cattle. Mothers also labored in the field, carrying their babes as well as their rude hoes and other tools. Then at night they cook for their husbands and wait on them at table before they eat themselves. The birth of a daughter was mourned over, nor were they reckoned in counting the family. It was deemed dishonorable to enquire after the health of a wife, nor might she speak to her husband before his parents, who, it will be remembered, lived in the same room. There was scarcely a husband who did not beat his wife, and such treatment yielded the natural fruit of bitter hate.

The change wrought by the grace of God appears in an incident that occurred in the Seminary in 1849. One of the older pupils was betrothed and when the ring was to be placed on her finger she could not be found. After long search she was heard in a retired part of the building humbly imploring the blessing of God on her new relation. Only those who have seen the reveling common on such occasions can appreciate the change in marriage ceremonies and entertainments which are now much more in accordance with the spirit of the Gospel.

In 1835, Heleneh, the sister of Mar Shimon, was the only woman who could read. Ask one " Would you like to read?" and the answer would be, "I am a woman," as though that settled it. Both sexes regarded it as immodest for a woman to read. All that was lovely and of good report was lacking in many. They were wronged, but also defiant, hateful and hating. Their outbursts of passion were awful to witness. The list of those who did not love their husbands was as large as that of those who beat their wives. Miss Fiske's pity for them became anguish when she found how low they were. They appealed to her as sent of the Virgin Mary to help them, and she had to answer, that she came not to save them from their husbands, but to show them how to be happy with them. To know how rapidly the human tongue can move, one must hear an Oriental woman in a fit of rage; one alone often drove off the tax-gatherers from a village after the men had fled. None who ever heard the stinging shrillness of their tongues, or looked on their frenzied gesticulations, would wonder why the Furies were painted as women. Their hair streams in the wind, and stones seem only the emphases of their yells. They are full as profane as the men. A dying convert, in her father's house, had to draw up the quilt over her head in order to pray unmolested for her revilers. Lying was as common as profanity, and stealing no less prevalent.

The following letter from Raheel (Rachel) shows the transformation effected by the Gospel in such women. It is written September 10, 1859, to the mother of Miss Fiske, in Shelburne, Mass.

My Dear Grandmother Hannah:—" Though I have never seen you, yet I must write to you, for I love all Miss Fiske's friends as I do my own and especially yourself. I thank you for all your love to me; blessings have thus reached me that were not given to others. When among us it was a disgrace for a girl to learn to read. God poured such love into your heart, as made you willing to send your daughter eight thousand miles to show our people that there is salvation for women. They used to dwell on those words of Solomon, 'One man among a thousand have I found, but a woman among all these have I not found'; but now they see that Christ died for women also. Many thanks for your self-denial all these years. I can appreciate it somewhat, for my own mother, if she did not see me for the five months of term time, mourned very much.

" It was certainly a sacrifice for Christ to come into this world, and for the Father to send His Son, when He knew all the agony there would be in His cup in this world of sin.

" You will see your daughter much changed from what she was fifteen years ago, but I know that when Christ shall sit upon His throne, judging the world, then all the sorrows of separation will seem to the Christian like the small dust of the balance, and especially to you when you see so many Nestorian girls on His right hand, whom you, through your daughter, were the means of bringing there, to have joyful life with Christ in His kingdom.

" I can never repay your love, but God can, and I ask Him to repay you in Heaven. I should never tire if I wrote to my dear mother Miss Fiske, every day, but this time I thought she would like me to write to you, and I hope that you will live to receive it. From your Grand-daughter whom you have not seen."

some three feet high. Black bread and yoghoort (sour curd) formed the supper. In such a crowd Mr. Stocking held evening service and Miss Fiske talked with the women till 10 o'clock. Then their hostess said, "now we will *settle* it." Her guest expected some family pacification, but it was only settling their places for the night. Some children were *settled* among some new hay in a manger; then one after another fell asleep on mats without mattress or pillow, and soon men and animals mingled in one discordant chorus of snoring. Miss Fiske had her carpet bag for a pillow, and before the lamp was put out, marked out for herself a route to the door between the sleepers. Fleas drove her out several times, and the cold as often drove her back, but sleep was impossible. Next day she thanked God for the pure air of the mountains, though the narrow path at times lay along the edge of a precipice; but her quarters that night were in striking contrast to the last, for they were in the home of one of her pupils, who welcomed her saying, "I heard where you were last night and know you had no sleep. Come right to my room, it is clean, and no one shall disturb you." Two hours of refreshing sleep preceded a dinner of fresh bread, nicely browned fish, honey from their own hives, and milk from their own flocks.

To keep her guest's room uncontaminated, Senum took her to another, where she met some three hundred women, who never heard before such words as she spoke of Christ and His salvation. And here we add, that now, some husbands provide a separate apartment for their brides, and need the word "home" to give expression to their mutual joy. Thoughtful preparation is also made for the hour of woman's suffering, and many hearts safely trust in the daughters of the Seminary.

CHAPTER III.

THE BEGINNINGS.

IF Nestorians were so prejudiced against the education of woman, how was that prejudice overcome? Mrs. Judith, wife of Dr. A. Grant, was a rare scholar before marriage, both in the classics and mathematics. In Persia she was soon at home in the Turkish. She read the ancient Syriac and acquired the vernacular with facility. She taught Mar Yohanan and other bishops English. And as they saw her turn to her Greek Testament whenever the English differed from the Syriac, they learned to honor womanhood. All her rare gifts were laid at the feet of her Saviour. And when such an one showed intense desire for the education of woman, prejudice fell before her. She taught her domestics to read. She mingled with both Christian and Moslem women, and did not rest till she had opened a school for girls. She began with only four. And, when her health forced her to leave the school room, her pupils came to her sick chamber. Her ready pencil prepared Syriac maps, and the *Missionary Herald* was indebted to her for the map of Oroomiah that so often appeared there, and in the Annual Reports. Her successors have often wondered at the power she put forth in behalf of the education of woman, and Mar Elias only voiced the feelings of all good men, when, after her death, he said: "As she has done so much for us, we want the privilege of digging her grave with our own hands."

After her, the school was cared for by Mr. Holladay, and

then passed into the hands of Dr. Wright, who had charge of it when Miss Fiske arrived, June 14, 1843. It was at that time only a day school, and contact with vice in the home greatly hindered its success. For that reason she sought to make it a boarding school, but it was a question whether parents would allow their daughters to spend the night under her roof. Still the mission appropriated money for the support of six pupils to be under its control for three years. Some doubted the possibility of the plan. Even Priest Abraham said: "I cannot bear the reproach of having my daughter live with you." Scarcely a girl twelve years of age was not betrothed, and years were devoted to preparation for the wedding. Miss Fiske wrote: "The first Syriac word I learned was *bratha* (daughter), and I often ask parents for their daughters. Mrs. Grant got day scholars, and I mean to devote at least five years to getting boarding scholars. I wonder that I am allowed to take her place." She spent the time between 3 o'clock and tea among the mothers, who often said: "Mrs. Grant did just as you do."

One day in August Mar Yohanan told her: "You get ready, and I find girls;" but October came and not one had been found. Looking out from her window one day, she saw him crossing the court leading a girl by each hand. One was Selby, his own niece, seven years of age, and the other, Hanee, three years older. Their outward appearance was not inviting, but it did not take her long to reach the door, where the bishop laid the little hands in hers, saying: "They be your daughters. No man take them from your hand." She, on her part, was glad to give them to the Lord Jesus. The number soon increased to six, though a fortnight after, two of them ran away. Ten years later she saw two women at a re-union of the school whom she did not know. They were the runaways, very sorry now, though their places had soon been filled.

The care of the school was much more wearing than its instruction, for it knew no intermission, day or night, on the Sabbath or through the week. When she went out she must take her pupils with her, for she dared not leave them alone; indeed, they had been allowed to come only on condition that they should lodge with her and go out only in her company.

Many difficulties constantly drove her to God for help. One was the extreme poverty of the people. In 1837, even in the snows of winter, few children wore shoes. One boy in Sabbath School wore nothing but a cotton shirt, though the missionary needed all his winter clothes to keep him warm. This poverty disinclined parents to earn bread for their children in school, hence the mission fed them for a while; but in 1844 Miss Fiske took the lead in declining to do this, and though some feared she would have to resume the practice, it never was resumed. The Seminary numbered twenty-two before the end of the year. In spite of the opposition of Mar Shimon, twenty-six entered at the opening of the next year and the number had increased to forty in 1845. In 1885 the whole number in attendance was forty-five.

A special difficulty grew out of the condition of women in Moslem Persia. Ladies can neither live alone nor appear alone in the streets. They need the shelter of mission families. Many a Moslem eye was on the girls as the Gospel developed in them new personal attractions. A nobleman once tried to take one to his harem, but the English Consul interposed. Eternity alone will reveal the vigilance such dangers involved. Any mishap in those early years might have broken up the school. In vacation it seemed strange to Miss Fiske to be able to sleep free from anxiety.

Another difficulty was the want of books. In 1843 she only had one, the Ancient Syriac Bible, and a few chapters of the New Testament in the vernacular. Then came a spelling book, mental and written arithmetic; a geography; also a Scripture spelling book and geography of the Bible. But the book most efficient for mental culture was the Bible in the vernacular. The New Testament appeared in 1846 and the Old in 1852, and so eager were the pupils for its possession that when the New Testament was offered as a prize for committing to memory the more than *one* thousand texts of the Scripture Catechism, some learned them all in three weeks, and their joy in obtaining it could hardly be expressed.

CHAPTER IV.

THE SEMINARY.

HAVING visited Mt. Holyoke Seminary, Mar Yohanan often said, "Of all colleges in America, Mt. Holyoke be the best, and when I see such an one here I (am ready to) die." Where the Gospel is unknown both social condition and education move on a lower level. A school where the alphabet is taught must climb far before its graduates stand on the same literary level with graduates among us and yet its course of study may be the best possible for it. If ragged untutored girls, leaping over the benches like wild goats, learn to study diligently, move gently, be kind to each other and respectful to their teachers, that of itself is a good education. And if besides this, the literary standard rises year by year what more can we ask?

To the original reading, writing, singing, and composition, have been added, grammar, arithmetic, geography, Scripture geography, physical geography, and theology, algebra, physics and astronomy, hygiene, history and moral science with oral instructions in physiology, chemistry and other branches. In languages, the scholars have studied English and Turkish, Persian and ancient Syriac. The marked ability of the pupils as writers is explained first of all by their thorough study of their own Bibles, and then by Miss Fiske's habit of translating some of our English classics, and practical religious works. They understood those free translations, and they influenced them more than the exact renderings of the press.

Baxter's Saints Rest poured red hot into a Syriac mould was more effective than after it had cooled and been filed into conformity to the original. An additional year has been added to the regular four years' course, besides a preparatory department requiring two years.

The cost to each pupil is very small. In 1853, it was only $18, including board, fuel, light and clothing in part, and this at first was paid by the mission, but gradually, as they were able to bear it, Miss Fiske laid the burden on them, so as to train them to sustain their own institutions as soon as possible. Doing more for them than is necessary only aggravates their poverty. When they began to clothe themselves, it was delightful to see the interest parents took in clothing their daughters, then they paid a trifle for tuition, and though at first the collection of the small sum cost more than its money value, yet, as an education of the people to care for themselves, it was beyond all price. Afterwards Miss Fiske and Miss Rice advanced along the same line, and her successors still go on toward the self support which is the goal of their desires. A mission can not be content with less self denial on the part of its beneficiaries than is practiced by its supporters at home.

Except from the mountains, none are received now who do not furnish their own clothing, bed and books. Most pay for tuition annually two tomans ($4.00), a few one toman ($2.00), and a very few five sahib krans (a sahib kran is twenty-five cents).

In 1886, Monday afternoon was devoted to sewing, and the girls learned to mend neatly. At the examination that year much interest was awakened by an exhibition of their handiwork to which the village women were invited. Girls dressed in neatly mended garments were commended much more than those daily seen wearing velvet dresses and at the same time ragged stockings.

n the matter of dress, furniture and diet, the aim was not to educate them out of sympathy with their people, but to give them such a standard of neatness as through them to lead their people upward by a healthy advance.

Miss Fiske had such a dread of the home influences that at first she sought to retain her pupils even through vacations, but she soon saw that both their health and usefulness suffered, and that to retain their sympathy with the people, and that of the people with them, the vacation must be spent at home. This opened the way for many delightful meetings with native women, in which the pupils rendered valuable aid. It also secured the co-operation of parents in promoting the good of their daughters. During her whole stay in Persia, fathers rarely disregarded her wishes for their daughters.

The poverty of the mission called for a domestic department in the Seminary, and, though girls ten years of age could not take charge of it, yet a beginning was made, but it required unspeakable labor and patience, for at first their work was much more of a hindrance than a help. Still it trained them to wait upon themselves, the influence of bad domestics was avoided, and as they could not walk out unprotected, the work took the place of out door exercise, and thus promoted health, while the pupils learned to be content in their humble homes, having formed habits of system, punctuality and neatness such as they could not otherwise have learned. At the same time all that was harmless in their home habits was left untouched.

At first, in their daily reports, no question was asked which the teacher herself could not answer, beginning with the single inquiry whether they had combed their hair that day. By degrees she added others as they were able to bear them. Under so gentle a search they may have deemed themselves very good, but they little suspected how much she did not dare to ask. After the revival, she could ask about things she did not know, and now, in this matter, they compare well with our own Seminaries. There is very little communication in the school-room. In 1852 there were only five failures on this point for four months, and those by new scholars. How many schools at home could show a better record?

Miss Fiske thus pictures a day's work in 1854. Waked by a bell at early dawn, in twenty minutes all are ready for their half hour of private devotion, during which the quiet is almost perfect. Then at family prayer in the school-room, besides reading Scripture and prayer, they sing a Syriac hymn, and some of them can repeat all the hymns in the hymn-book. (In 1862 there were two-hundred.) Soon after this comes breakfast. Then all attend to their morning work, followed by an hour of quiet study in their rooms. At 8:45, Miss Fiske enters the school-room and offers the opening prayer. Then the older pupils recite in Daniel, after that the others come in from reciting in another room, and soon recess in the yard makes all fresh again. The younger classes then study with Miss Fiske the life of Christ, and it is delightful to hear their own fresh thoughts concerning the blessed Saviour. His journeys are traced on maps prepared by themselves. After this, one class recites ancient Syriac to Yonan, and another in physiology goes out to Miss Rice, leaving Miss Fiske with the older girls and their compositions. The present topic for these is "Christ in the old Testament." After a general exercise of fifteen minutes, comes the noon recess of one and a half hours for lunch and recreation. The last fifteen minutes of this are devoted to a prayer meeting.

In the afternoon Miss Rice has charge of the school. The first hour is given to writing, or astronomy. Geography follows till recess, and, after that, singing or spelling. The last hour Miss Fiske hears a lesson on the Epistle to the Hebrews, studied in connection with the Old Testament. At the same hour, Miss Rice has a lesson in Judges, and then come the daily reports, and an hour before supper is given to calls. After supper is cleared away, comes recess, followed by evening prayer. Then an hour for study, and half an hour for private devotion closes the day.

Saturday is for washing and mending, and the girls are busy all day long. Before sunset all repair to the school room, to see if everything is in order. Half an hour before supper sees all finished, and after leaving the supper table everything is arranged for the morning, and all have a quiet half hour in their rooms. Then the school is divided into two prayer meetings, each led by a teacher, in which absent ones are remembered, also the seminaries in Constantinople, South Hadley and Oxford (Ohio). All retire from these meetings to their half hour, as they call it, and before 9 o'clock all is quiet.

On Sabbath they rise at 5:30, and dress for the day. Morning prayer is at 6:30, then breakfast, followed by morning work. After that they study their Sunday-school lesson. At 9:30 comes Syriac service in the chapel, followed by a Sunday school of some two-hundred pupils, in which two-thirds of the members of the Seminary are teachers. The afternoon service begins at 2 o'clock, and the Bible lesson an hour before supper, though some are called earlier to teach the women who come in. At the supper table is evening prayers, and at 7 o'clock the teachers go to the English prayer-meeting, while each room has what they call a family prayer-meeting by itself. After that, the teachers converse with any who want to see them, and this hour often witnesses some, for the first time, submitting to God.

Let us view the Seminary from a native standpoint. Esli, one of the teachers, wrote to Miss Fiske in 1859: "We have pleasant seasons of prayer in our school this winter, and we trust some have been born again; my circle of girls in the kitchen works well and keeps it clean. Should you drop in you would find everything in order. On Wednesday we scour the shelves and doors. I went to my village in vacation. Our prayer-meetings were delightful, and I enjoyed much, praying with the women alone. In the school we have studied Ezra in connection with Haggai and Zechariah, and are now in Nehemiah. In the New Testament, we are on the third journey of Paul, and are nearly through Scripture geography.'

These extracts are from a journal she kept in 1860:

"Feb. 1. To-day a part of the girls wrote on anger, and others had for a topic, 'the Gospel.'

"3d. John was here to-day writing to Mount Holyoke Seminary, and attended our noon prayer-meeting. In the afternoon, Deacon Joseph preached from the words: 'King of Kings, and Lord of Lords.' In the evening Mr. Coan sang with us.

"9th. A blessed morning, some are very thoughtful. This appeared in the quiet at table and the silence in the kitchen. The work was done earlier and better than usual. During the study hour, the voice of prayer sounded sweetly in every room. While walking in the yard, and when they came in, the girls were very quiet. While Hanee prayed at our noon meeting some wept. When Miss Rice dismissed us none moved, all were bowed on their desks weeping. She then called for prayer, and while I prayed all were in tears. All the rules have been well kept to-day. This evening communicants met with Miss Rice, the rest with Martha. Hanee asked us to pray for Rachel, and I asked prayers for Hannah and Parangis who are in my room."

Miss M. S. Rice has kindly furnished the following names of the teachers in the seminary, with the dates of their service:

Fidelia Fiske,	from June 1843,	to July 1858.
Mary Susan Rice,	" Nov. 1847,	" May 1869.
Aura J. Beach,	" July 1860,	" Sept. 1862.
Mrs. Sarah J. Rhea,	" 1865,	" 1869.
N. Jennie Dean,	" Oct. 1868,	still there.
Mary K. Van Duzee	" 1875,	" "

Harriet N. Crawford, and Lucy M. Wright were connected with the Seminary in the winter of 1864–'65.

Deacon Siyad was native teacher from the beginning of Mrs. Grant's labors, down to the coming of Miss Dean.

Malik Yonan taught from 1847 to 1860.

The first class that graduated (3) became teachers.

Rachel and Martha taught from 1858 to 1864.

Hoshebo has taught for twenty years.

The writer would have liked to give as full an account of the labors of the successors of Miss Fiske, as of hers, but several reasons prevent this. There is not the same material for so full a record of their work. In many things it would be a mere repetition of what has been already told, and last but not least, this is an abridgment of a larger work, and there is hardly room for the few words that seek to give the reader some idea of the work as it has gone forward since she rested from her labors.

CHAPTER V.

EARLY LABORS FOR WOMEN.

THE teachers of the Seminary labored for mothers as well as for daughters, and never felt that they gave them too much of their time. At first the women felt that they could not attend the same service with men, but Miss Fiske induced a few to come to her room at the same hour, and as she was not yet a proficient in Syriac (1844), she had a missionary conduct the service. The first day only five came, but soon the number grew to forty; on the third Sabbath, she found one bowed to the dust with a sense of her sinfulness. When Miss Fiske prayed with her she repeated every word very softly, and so intense were her feelings that she rose from her knees covered with perspiration. She confessed that her life had been one of opposition to God, and that no outward observances could procure forgiveness. She was pointed to the Lamb of God who taketh away sin, and at length, to use her own words, "I was praying, and the Lord poured peace into my heart." From being one of the most turbulent of her sex, she became noted for her gentleness and general consistency. This first enquirer died afterwards, trusting peacefully in her Savior.

Miss Fiske also went to other places. One Sabbath she went to Geog Tapa with Mr. Stoddard. It was afternoon, and she was very tired. After the constant strain of the week, during which the burden of her care knew no intermission, not even at night, came the labor of the Sabbath. She had already conducted one prayer-meeting, and taught a Sabbath school, and as she sat on the earthen floor of the church, without any support for her back, it seemed as though nature must give way. Then she thought, "after this service comes my meeting with the women," and she felt wholly unequal to the effort. As she sat, longing for rest, God sent it in a way she had not looked for. A Nestorian woman saw how tired she was, and sitting down close behind her, bade her lean on her, "But what can you lean on?" was the reply. "I could not be so selfish." Then the strong woman put her arm round her and drawing her back said: "IF YOU LOVE ME, LEAN HARD," and she yielded and was refreshed. Her person was a soft resting place for the body, her kindness was a greater refreshment to the spirit. And then Miss Fiske seemed to hear the Master repeat the words: "If you love *me*, lean hard," and she leaned on him also, rejoicing that unlike the woman, he was not wearied by the burden. She felt that the Lord Jesus spoke through that woman, and her heart overflowed with the peace of God. That hour with the women was an unusual feast, and after sunset she rode back six miles to her home. She wondered that there was no reaction; neither that night, nor next day, and she went many days resting on those sweet words: "If you love me, lean hard," nor was she alone refreshed, but many others have also drank of this fountain in the wilderness, and shared her comfort.

Some of her first efforts to interest women in the Bible were amusing in the manner in which difficulties were overcome.

She would sit down among them on the floor, read a verse, and then question them to see if they understood it: for example, after reading about the Creation she asked "Who was the first man?" They answered, "What do we know: we are women;" equivalent in English to "We are donkeys." Then she read again "The Lord God called unto Adam," and asked "Who did God speak to?" Again no answer. Then she made them repeat the name of Adam over and over till they remembered it. This set them to listening, and listening to thinking. The machinery was there, but so rusty that it required all her skill and patience to make it move. The least movement, however, was great gain. Another lesson would take up Eve, (Syriac Hawa, meaning Life.) She began: "Is not that a pretty name? and wouldn't you like to know that you had a great-grandmother called Life? Now that was the name of our first mother, both yours and mine." Faces previously stolid lighted up after that, whenever the preacher mentioned the names of our first parents. One would nudge another and say, "Didn't you hear? He said Adam," or "Hawa," as the case might be. This was in the city; but in the country villages it was certainly no better.

In the summer of 1844 Mr. Stocking proposed a visit to Ardishai. So one horse carried the tent, another Mr. Stocking's children in baskets balanced on either side of the pack saddle; and a third miscellaneous baggage, and besides these were the animals they rode. The first night the tent was pitched on one of the threshing floors of Geog Tapa, but, as American ladies were a novelty in Ardishai, in that village it was pitched on one of the flat roofs, to be out of the reach of annoyance.

It was Miss Fiske's first day in a large village, and she became quite exhausted in her long talks with the women. Then the mosquitoes allowed no rest at night, and morning brought back the crowd as persistent as the tinier assailants during the darkness. When Mr. Stocking preached in the church the women sat close to their strange sisters, handling and commenting on their foreign dresses. At the close Priest Abraham, without any authority, announced that Miss Fiske would preach in the afternoon. Mr. Stocking, however, took her place and preached to some six hundred women and half as many children. They were so noisy that at no time were there less than half a dozen voices competing with the preacher. When he closed many cried, "Now let Miss Fiske preach." So he left her to their tender mercies. She told them that when she knew their language better she would talk with them, but she could not speak at the same time with them, for God had given her a very small voice and her words could no more mingle with theirs than oil and water. They said "We will be silent if you will come and preach." Months passed and she returned. Hundreds came to hear her, but they were not silent. When she began they began, and if she asked them to be quiet, each commanded her neighbor to be still, and the louder the uproar the louder were the orders. At length she said, "I cannot speak more until you put your fingers on your mouths." All fingers went up and she proceeded. "I have a story to tell, but if one finger goes down I must stop." Instantly muffled voices on all sides cried, "Be still, so that we can hear the story;" and the four hundred women were silent. "Once there was an old woman; I did not know her ; nor my father ; nor, I think, my grandfather, but he told me"——. Here began many questions about said grandfather, but the fingers were ordered up; for they should hear no more if they talked about him. —"Now, this woman talked in meeting, and, after many reproofs, she was forbidden to go to church. She promised to do better; but, poor soul, she could not be still. Then, as soon as she heard her own voice, she cried: 'Oh, I have spoken in meeting! What shall I do! Why, I keep on speaking and cannot stop!" By this time their fingers were pressed on their lips, and none uttered a sound. Having thus secured silence she read to them from the Gospel about Mary, talked and prayed with them, and they went away still and thoughtful. This incident gives a vivid picture of woman as she was in Persia, and the tact needed to secure a first hearing for the truth. In March, 1850, Miss Rice met nearly three hundred women in the same church; some awakened, and a few already hopefully converted.

In July, 1851, Mr. Stocking and family and Misses Fiske and Rice, with others, spent the vacation in Gawar, moving in tents like the ancient patriarchs. They first pitched their camp near Memikan. The women came to see them frequently, and few left without some idea of the way of life. The native helpers here were unwearied in labors, and sometimes woke the others in the morning with their prayers. On Sabbath, after morning service, the women came to the tents to receive instruction. In the evening, one whose son, a member of the Boys' Seminary, had died in February, brought her youngest daughter to give to them in his stead. She said "Guwergis has gone to Heaven; you led him there; and we now intrust to you our little daughter." The father said, as his tears glistened in the moonlight, "I shall soon re-join him. My trust in Jesus grows stronger every day." The mention of the son's name secured attention at ce from all, to any word spoken about his Saviour.

On Monday they left for Ishtazin on mules, as horses could not travel the frightful paths. At another time, on the same road, the saddle-girth broke and Miss Fiske fell, but providentially was unhurt. Sometimes they climbed, or more perilous still, descended a steep, rocky stair, or were hid in the clouds that hung around the peaks above then. Now they passed under large detached rocks, that seemed ready to crush them, and now under solid cliffs that suggested the shadow of a great rock in a weary land. In the valley were water-falls; little plats rescued with much labor from the waste; fruits, and such a variety of flowers, that it seemed as if three seasons had united to supply them. The eye rested on what appeared to be silver threads hanging from distant summits, but were in fact, torrents dashing headlong down the rocks, yet so far off that no sound reached the ear.

The party stopped at Oŏreya on a flat roof shaded by a splendid walnut tree. The people brought mulberries and apples, while a more substantial meal was prepared. After supper all adjourned to the church-yard, and there in the moonlight eagerly listened to the Gospel. The silence of night was broken only by the voice of the preacher, and the surrounding rocks seemed to repeat joyfully the unwonted sounds. Yonan preached from the words "Jesus went about all Galilee——preaching the Gospel of the Kingdom." He asked whether Christ did right in this. "Certainly," was their reply. "Then as He did, so must His people do. When we cease to do this, think that we have apostatized to Islam, for Christians cannot but go from place to place to preach the Gospel." To appreciate this, the reader must remember that Mar Shimon had forbidden his people to receive the missionaries because they preached the Gospel. Then he gave an account of the doctrines that Jesus preached, bringing out the very marrow of the Gospel. Khamis followed with an impassioned exhortation. He had been considered a good preacher before, but here, in his native mountains, he went beyond himself.

The next forenoon was filled up by personal conversation with those who never heard such truths before. In the evening very earnest attention was given to an open-air service in Boobawa. The following Sabbath, besides two services in Memikan there was preaching in three other villages. In Chardewar, the home of Priest Dunkha, his daughter Sanum, just arrived, was already full of work. One Sabbath almost every woman in the place had come to hear her, and she said she could not ask a better field in which to work for Christ.

From Memikan they went to Darawe, where the people would hardly allow them to pitch their tent; yet even here the power of Christian love was felt. Neighboring villagers wondered at their going there, and still more at their being able to remain. At Keyat the kindness of the people was the more grateful for the contrast.

Next Sabbath Yonan preached to about two hundred people at Sanawar, where were many refugees from Saat. Their camp was a circle of huts, where spinning and weaving was going on as well as cooking; but the women at once left their work to welcome Misses Fiske and Rice. Some of them had heard the Gospel in Mosul. One widow, though unable to read, showed a spiritual acquaintance with the truth. When sin was spoken of: "Yes," said she, "we were all shapen in iniquity, as David testifies." When asked if she expected to be saved, she replied: "I am very far from God, yet my only hope is in the wounds of Christ. If I stand penitently beneath His cross I hope that though my sins are red like scarlet yet they shall become as white as snow." It was inspiring in a region where they looked only for darkness, to find the light streaming through from another mission. It was a foretaste of the time when the voice of one watchman should reach to another on those mountain tops. Some years later they heard that this stranger sister held fast her trust until she fell asleep in Jesus.

If this was true so far back as 1851 we should expect similar heralds of the dawn since then, and the Oroomiah report of the work for women in 1885 tells us that Elia (Elias) of Buhtan (Layard writes Boktan), a district in the mountains east of Jezireh has taken for a wife Rukhamee (See Hos. ii:1) daughter of Priest Mikhael, one of the early helpers in Mosul. She was educated at Mardin, and for several years has been teaching there. She is a most valuable addition to our force in that part of the field. Though she spoke Arabic only, before her marriage, then she began the study of the Syriac, and can now conduct a Bible class in that language. She has taken hold of the work with much interest and energy. Rakhamee, wife of Hammo, in the same district, has come here with him to qualify themselves for more efficient labor for Christ. She is gentle and humble, but quick to respond to anything she is asked to do for Jesus' sake. Three pupils of the Seminary are now living at Buhtan, and the women keep up regular Friday evening prayer meetings in the villages of Rukhamee and Rakhamee.

As a companion picture to this, take a visit of the same persons, with thirteen of the pupils, in June, 1852, to Gavalan, the home of Mar Yohanan. It lies at the northern end of the plain, forty miles from Oroomiah. On the East the blue waters of the lake stretch away to the South in quiet beauty. In the gorgeous hues of sunset, or when reflecting the red rays of the full moon they remind one of "the sea of glass mingled with fire." In the long summer days the breeze from the lake is very grateful, and the evening air from the mountains makes sleep refreshing.

Mar Yohanan gave the school free use of two rooms during its stay. In the court a large tent was dining room and divan khaneh (reception room) by day and dormitory at night. An adjoining house made a good recitation room. Here the regular work of the school went on, and while, in the evening, the men found their way to Mr. Stocking, the women came to Misses Fiske and Rice. At the last meeting with them nearly forty were present, listening with quiet interest. On the Sabbath the walls of the tent were lifted outward, so as to admit the air and exclude the sun; thus forming a pleasant chapel. In the forenoon it was thronged. The boys' school of the village sat around its teacher. The girls' school was known by the smoothness of the hair, the whiteness of the face, and general neatness. The Seminary crowded close to its teachers, and still all could not get under the tabernacle. Mr. Stocking preached in the forenoon, and in the afternoon was Sabbath school. Each pupil of the Seminary had a class and seemed quite at home in the work. They visited their scholars during the week; and in the school, if the teacher was zealous in her work, the class showed no less interest in being taught. With the same diversity of character as with us, the school showed a greater variety of lessons. Some were in the Old Testament and some in the New. One class was just able to read and another had to be orally taught, while a class of Armenians recited in Turkish.

On the third Sabbath women and children had vanished, for a report had gone abroad that all this labor was only preparing the way to carry them off to America, but visits during the week dispelled their fears, and this pleasant work went on till September.

CHAPTER VI.

REVIVALS.

IT is time to go back a few years and give some account of the Revivals in this mission. The first one seemed to burst forth suddenly like a fountain in the desert. Yet as that is connected with channels below the surface, so was this with an extended preparatory work. For years there had been a diligent inculcation of Gospel truth, and a few individuals had been converted. Deacon John was one of these as far back as 1844. Even among the unrenewed, there was a great difference between communities where missionaries had labored, and those not so favored. The truth had produced a marked change in the habits, intelligence and general appearance of the pupils in the Seminaries. They could no longer trust in their fasts, and they had an intellectual apprehension of the way of salvation through Christ. Those best instructed were the first to come to him, and have since lived the most consistent lives, for God sanctifies through the truth. Then the very delay of the blessing called forth more earnest prayer from the husbandmen who were waiting for precious fruit, being patient over it until it received the early and latter rain. Besides, the diminished numbers of the missionaries and the opposition of Mar Shimon shut them up to God as their only hope, while among their native helpers the army of Gideon was being rapidly thinned out. The feeling was very strong. "All our springs are in God." One said late in 1845, "God never formed a soul which Christ cannot redeem from the power of sin. I know these people are sunk in sin, but Christ died to save them, and He shall see in them the travail of his soul, if we are only humble and faithful enough to lead them to him."

One day in the autumn of 1845, Mr. Stocking, Miss Fiske and Deacon John were riding together when the Deacon asked in English. "If we ever have a revival here, what shall we call it?" Mr. Stocking replied, "First get it, then we will find a name." And when it came the Nestorians at once called it "an awakening." Toward the end of the year Deacon John was more active in labor, and earnest in prayer. The teachers in the Seminaries thought not so much of the present character of their pupils, as of the power of God to make them like himself and they labored expecting a blessing. The first Monday of January, 1846, was a day of fasting and prayer. Miss Fiske at morning devotions told her pupils that many were praying for them that day in a distant land, and dismissed them to their studies, Two, Sanem and Sarah, lingered behind, and she said. "Did you not understand me?" They did not answer and she saw they were in tears. "Have you heard bad news?" Still no answer, but when near enough, they said in a low voice. "May we have to-day to care for our souls?" Sarah added, "Perhaps next year I shall not be here." They had no closet, but they made one for themselves in the wood cellar, and spent the day looking unto Jesus. Their teacher did not know where they had gone, till after the death of Sarah, the survivor told her.

Sabbath evening, January 18, at the English prayer meeting, words were few, but the prayers carried the pupils to Jesus, and laid them at his feet. Mr. Stoddard was asked if he saw tokens of interest among his boys, for a while his heart was too full to speak, and then he said, "I should expect them, if I felt as I ought," and passed out. All were struck by his manner, so earnest and so humble. He retired to his study, called John and proposed that every day they make one pupil a subject of special prayer and labor, and begin that night with Yakob. They prayed for him, and then he said. "I want to talk to him to-night. We don't know what may be on the morrow; call him." He came expecting to be reproved for bad behavior that day, but when Mr. Stoddard kindly bade him sit down, and took his hand saying. "Have you ever thought that you had a soul to be saved or lost," he broke down at once, and confessed that the school had combined to shut out the subject from their thoughts, but were in fact so agitated that if one of them came to Christ he thought all would follow. Then the good man, who had mourned because he could see no impression from the sermon that day, thanked God and took courage. On Monday he conversed with another and he also went away to pray. At the recitation they both had to leave the room. "It is God," was the word that passed from seat to seat, and at noon they got together to discuss the situation. One proposed to put down the work, but Yonan said, "I don't want to be a Christian but I am afraid to oppose this. If it is the work of God we cannot put it down, if not, we need only let it alone." Nothing more was said but some of them were soon on their knees in prayer. In the evening Mr. Stoddard sent for two of the leaders in the opposition. Yonan was one of them and told afterwards that Mr. Stoddard said : "If you refuse to be saved yourself, I beg you not to hinder others, and eternity so opened up before me, that I was ready to sink. I longed for some one to speak to me of a way of escape. I could not sleep, for I saw but a step between me and death." Thursday evening another came deeply agitated, and after conversation he was left to pray alone, and that night he could not sleep. Next morning conversing with Mr. Stoddard he seemed to submit, and find rest.

On Monday evening Miss Fiske invited those willing to come to Christ at once, to come to her room at 5 o'clock. Before that hour, many were praying for themselves. Just then, she heard for the first time, what was taking place among the boys, and she turned to find five of her girls in the same condition. All the missionaries were untiring in labor, and every day brought out more of those who were taught of God. Wednesday evening, after a sermon from the words: "Behold I stand at the door and knock," no member of the boys' seminary left his seat. After a few personal words they were dismissed, but their feelings were so intense, that they came to the study till near midnight, when, utterly exhausted, their teacher retired.

Thursday evening the teachers of both seminaries were busy till midnight. During this week the teachers' rooms were so occupied by the pupils for prayer, that their owners could hardly get them for their own devotions. The girls often woke Miss Fiske in the morning, standing by her bedside, with some question about the way of life. When a new room had been fitted up in the girls' seminary that autumn, the first time Mr. Stoddard saw it, he said: "May it be consecrated to the Lord for ever," and on Friday evening, when both schools met in it, Christ seemed to take possession. Seldom has a company been so under the influence of things unseen. Christ himself seemed to speak through his servants, and this and that one entered into union with his Saviour. At the close of the week, ten were trusting in Christ, and on the Sabbath many strong men bowed down. Priest Eshoo, who had been watching others, now looked within. He had always scorned the weakness of tears, but now he wept aloud. Deacon Tamo, also, whose levity had so tried Mr. Stoddard, that he asked: "Can it be that he is allowed to come here and hinder the work?" now trembled for fear, and after Mr. Stoddard had prayed with him, said, with streaming eyes: "Thank you, for caring for my soul."

During the next week, most of the pupils in both seminaries were under deep conviction, with a strong tendency toward undue excitement. One evening, a score of boys rolled on the floor, groaning and crying aloud. At prayers, Mr. Stocking asked if any had seen the Nazloo river near its source. Surprised by the question, a few answered "Yes." "Was there much water in it?" Wondering yet more, the answer was, "No." "Did it make much noise?" "Yes, very much." "After it entered the plain was it deep and broad?" "Yes, it was full of water." "And was it more noisy?" "No, it was very quiet and still." He then said that he had hoped God had showed them the evil of their hearts, but their noise and confusion led him to fear there was no depth to their experience. The effect was wonderful. From many a closet that night was heard the prayer: "Lord make me to know my heart, and let me not be like that noisy river." The noisy excitement became deep contrition. Their feelings were not less intense, but more gentle, because more spiritual. The converts had much feeling, but little experience in giving that feeling expression, and in the freshness of emotion, like little children, they yielded to every impulse. If under conviction, that found free expression. If they hoped they were forgiven, that, too, at once found utterance.

There was wonderful transparency, and a tendency to excitement that needed careful handling. Sometimes they needed to be hindered from praying together.

For three weeks few came to the Seminary. It was like one protracted Sabbath. Every corner was consecrated to prayer; but after that, visitors came, and then the converts became helpers in Christ Jesus. Often a dozen women spent the night there, and then the large room became a dormitory. The teacher often staid with them till near midnight, and then could hear them praying the remainder of the night.

In both Seminaries as many as fifty gave evidence of conversion before the March vacation. When they left, their cry was: "Pray for us amid our temptations at home." One little girl said: "Can a new-born lamb be thrown into the snow and live? and can we live?" Thank God, most of them did live, and shall live forever with Him who gave His life for them.

Mr. Stoddard was abundant in labors. He wrote out his sermons carefully in English, but in the Syriac idiom. He also excelled in labor with individuals. The first enquirer became such while he pressed home upon him his guilt. After conversing he always prayed with one, and had him do the same, and after he had gone, again commended him to God. He kept a record of every case in a book, and when he began with a man he followed him up. He divided thirty converts into three classes, and met each of them twice a week. It was a great joy to him when they took part in meetings, and they did that as often as once a week (No wonder his strength was not equal to his zeal and love). He had great tact in setting others to work for Christ. He taught his pupils to work as well as pray, and assigned definite work to them, not only among schoolmates and visitors, but also among those indisposed to go to church. Once when three-fourths of the school were rejoicing in Christ, he brought in others, just to furnish work for them. It is needless to add that he himself was happy in his work.

The converts in the Girls' Seminary, after spending the summer of 1846 at home exposed to much temptation, returned all save one, established in Christian character. Their friends bore witness to their prayerfulness and cheerful obedience, and their influence on others was beneficial. For a while in the autumn, the school was broken up by cholera, but though hundreds died around them, after two months all were spared to meet again. Soon the converts were unusually earnest in prayer for the rest, and at once the answer came. The first awakened was Moressa, who had received much instruction from Mrs. Grant and Mr. Stocking. For a week her convictions were very deep, and soon others came through a like experience to rest in Christ.

The first token of a work of grace in 1849 was the unusual seriousness of Deacon John. He had been reading Pike's Guide to Young Disciples, and the chapter on backsliding moved him deeply. This was followed by earnest effort for others, and many converts passed with him through deep searching of heart into a new consecration to God. For days some of them wept and prayed. Their past unfaithfulness to Christ and souls was the great grief of many. One who had wept thus bitterly herself, was fitted to lead others back to God. Her labors were incessant, and in the reduced state of the Mission the labors of these converts were very helpful, though their Oriental ardor needed careful guiding, to preserve their health and efficiency. In Geog Tapa, during a short vacation, their daily meetings for women had an attendance of from thirty to one hundred.

Many were glad to learn the Gospel even from children.

In Seir. besides the labors of the members of the Boys' Seminary, Sanum and Moressa labored among the women. They wrote to Miss Lovell's school at Constantinople:

"What shall we tell you, beloved, of the great love God has shown us? For two months we have been happier than we ever were before. The work of the Lord has also begun in the villages. May you see greater wonders among your own people than we see here. In Seir, which contains nineteen houses, God has visited every family, and two of us were sent there, not because we were fit for the work, for we are deficient in godly knowledge, and every qualification, but because God sometimes chooses the ignorant and weak to do him service; and what shall we tell you of the wonders God showed among these poor women? There was no time in which they did not cry: 'Woe unto us! We are lost! What shall we do?' When we asked them to pray with us they prayed as those do who are taught of God. We wondered at them very much. One woman beat her head with both hands, crying: 'Oh, my sins! They are so great! There is no forgiveness!' We tried to reason with her but she would not hear. If we took her hands from her head she beat her breast. She said: 'You told me, the other day, to go to Christ, but I am such a sinner that He will not receive me!' With difficulty we induced her to hear of the great mercy of the Lord.

"On one occasion we heard a man, perhaps ninety years old, praying in the stable, and his wife in the house. We told them how ready Christ was to dwell with them, poor as they were. The tears rolled down their wrinkled faces and made our own hearts burn within us. The man prayed with us as if Christ stood right before him.

"Meetings were held several times a day, and after them prayer might be heard on all sides, in the houses and stables. Every family now has morning and evening worship."

In this revival the native helpers felt deep anxiety for their unconverted wives. The first visit that Siyad and Yonan made at their homes were blessed to the conviction of their companions, who soon came to the school begging to be taught the way of life. The former had been such a bitter opposer that her frequent visits were always dreaded. But now her convictions deepened day by day till they were overwhelming, then, as she said, "the Saviour found her," and she was at rest. Three children and a daughter-in-law came with her to Christ—witnesses, both to her consistency and her faithful efforts to do them good.

Yonan had been married by force two years before, while his heart was set on another. It was a sore trial, but in these matters parents in Persia have everything their own way, and his great desire was to see his wife a Christian. At midnight he was often heard praying for her, and now the answer came. Miss Fiske never forgot the first time she heard her praying with her husband. She then saw new meaning in the words "They believed not for joy." She became very active among the women in her village, and when her father-in-law forbade prayer in his house she took her little company behind the church, where the bleak winds of February did not chill their devotion.

Khanumjan, the mother of John, though past seventy years of age, entered into the work with great zeal. She took the aged women one by one into her closet, that then and there they might accept the Saviour. Though unable to read herself, she encouraged those who did, providing food for such as went to preach in the villages. No wonder she told one: "Three years ago I saw Christ, but now He sits by my side all day long."

In this revival there was more encouragement to labor for

women than ever before. After January 15th, the Seminary was constantly full of enquirers. Day and night it was consecrated by the prayers of women seeking their Saviour. On the Sabbath many from the villages staid there between services. Sometimes their feelings were so intense that they could eat nothing but the bread of life.

Degala was so noted for vice that the Nestorians called it Sodom. The first convert there was a young man employed in the Seminary. One day he came, asking if the teacher would receive a petition. Supposing he wanted money, she replied: "Tell me what it is." He at once broke down, and sobbed out: "My village is lost! My family is perishing, and their blood is on my neck. Let me go and beg forgiveness for my wicked example, and urge them to flee from the wrath to come." He went, and next morning brought his wife and other women to be taught. A week after this Deacon Tamo found several enquirers in that village, and one woman in great agony for her sins. She had been so vile that scarce any one would be seen with her. Next day she came to the seminary and threw herself at the feet of Miss Fiske, crying: "Do tell me what to do, or where to go, to get rid of my sins." She was pointed to Christ, and one moment her feet would rest on the rock, the next a fresh wave of conviction swept her into the raging sea. She was asked to pray, and though she had not in all her life heard ten prayers, her fervent petitions showed that the Spirit helped her infirmities. She dated back her convictions to a word spoken in the Seminary by a stranger, who one day seized her hand as soon as she entered, saying: "My sister, we are all lost; we must repent or perish." She could not get the words out of her mind, and from that hour sought Christ until she found Him, and then bore reviling so meekly as to win others also to her Saviour. She is now a most attractive Christian.

After the revival in 1850, conversions occurred each year, but not in so marked a manner as in 1849. In 1856 the pupils were very studious and kind to each other, but winter was over before the diminished number of believers began to grow. On Sabbath evening, February 18, Miss Fiske was in that desponding state that sometimes follows intense but unsatisfied desire. At such times feeling seems to die of sheer exhaustion. All had retired, and she was alone. Her thoughts brooded over the state of things, but she had not strength to carry her charge to Christ. The clock struck 11, and there was a knock on the door—must she see another face? She opened, and there stood a pupil, not so insensible as she had thought. Struck by the looks of her teacher, she asked very tenderly: "Are you very tired?" "Not very—why do you ask?" "Because I can not sleep for thinking of our school, and I thought perhaps you would help me to pray." The spell was broken. The dry fountain flowed afresh, and with a full heart she said: "Come in, thou blessed of the Lord." As an angel from Heaven, that dear pupil brought strength to her, and together they carried the whole family to Jesus, and then retired in the peace of God, which passeth understanding. "Could ye not watch with me one hour?" were the words given her in the morning, and hardly had she repeated them at prayers before three, in different parts of the room, were weeping. She said little, for she felt it safer to go and tell Jesus. All day long the feeling was subdued and tender: no one asked a question but there was stillness at the table and in the rooms. The work was done well, but in silence, and the voice of prayer was gentle. Tuesday passed in like stillness. Toward evening she said:

"If any one wants to seek first the Kingdom of God, I will see her at half past eight o'clock." At that hour one entered alone, and then another and another, till the room was full. She closed the door, and still they came, till she looked around on twenty-three bowing down in silence. She felt that they needed to hear God rather than man, and the parable of the prodigal son seemed to come that evening fresh from the lips of Jesus. Wednesday each lesson was recited promptly and well, but tears blurred many a page, and at recess many went to be alone with God. At eleven o'clock, when Dr. Perkins came in to sing with them, all began to sing 'Bartimeus,' but one after another stopped singing till the voice of the leader was alone. He took up the Bible lying before him, and read the same parable and offered prayer. The noon recess had to be lengthened, for the teachers could not bear to call the pupils from private communion with God.

The mission met that afternoon in the seminary and spent the time mostly in prayer. A very deep and silent work followed, noted for humble penitence and simple dependence on the Saviour. Most of those twenty-three began to hope in the mercy of God through Christ.

It did good to the Nestorians to find three children of missionaries among the converts, for when they saw them also come as lost sinners to Christ, they realized as never before that the children of believers also must be born again.

The English embassador passed through the city at this time, and though he and his suite visited the Seminary, not only did the pupils do credit to the school in their examinations, but their relish for spiritual things was not impaired by the episode, which in the East would ordinarily have crowded out all other thoughts.

The Seminary was again blessed in 1857, and in each of the four years that followed, up to 1862, it had enjoyed twelve revivals, and it should be mentioned to the praise of divine grace, that two-thirds of those connected with it have in the judgment of charity been created anew in Christ Jesus.

CHAPTER VII.

FIRST FRUITS.

LET us now turn back to take a view of some of the converts of these revivals.

The first to ask the way to heaven and to enter there, was Sarah, daughter of Priest Eshoo, of Gawar. Though at first, like other fathers, he regretted her coming into the world, yet her strong attachment to him so won his love, that in 1835, when the family fled from the destruction of their village by the Kurds, he carried her on his back as the mother carried the younger sister. They stopped for a time in Degala, and subsisted by begging. The mental gifts of the father, however, brought him into notice, and one day the question of Mrs. Grant, "Have you any daughters for our school?" revived a half-forgotten desire that Sarah might learn to read, and in 1841, when she was ten years old, he sent her to the seminary. She was dark eyed and slender; also in feeble health. Yet though often a great sufferer, she applied herself so diligently that she soon became the best scholar in the school. The Bible was the principal text book, and she was their walking concordance. Her knowledge of the scripture teachings was even more marked, and under Mrs. Harriet Stoddard she learned to sing hymns very sweetly. Still she was without Christ, and her health caused much anxiety. On the first Monday of 1346, she said to Sanum, who she knew was also thoughtful, "Sister, we ought to turn to God. Shall we ever find a better time than when they are praying for us?" Together they devoted the day to seek the Lord, as we have seen and from that time she never turned back. As soon as she found peace for herself, she sought to lead others to Christ. Weak as she was, she never shrunk from labor. She spent hours every day in her closet, and sacredly used all her time for Christ. She had much to do with the conversion of the twenty that followed after her to the Saviour before she died, and she did much for the women who visited the Seminary. Miss Fiske never knew a young person more anxious to do good. Both pupils and visitors loved to have Sarah tell them the way. They said they could see it more plainly when she told them. Her teacher often remonstrated with her for her excessive labors, but she felt that she must be about her Father's business while the day lasted. Her anxiety for her father began with her own interest in salvation, and his feelings were soon so tender that he could not speak of them without tears. Sarah was the first to know that he had found peace, and his first word with her on spiritual things was telling her that he had found Christ. He was not prepared to find her so full of humble and holy joy. Next day, when urged to seek the salvation of his family, he replied, "Sarah knows more about it than I do." Their previous strong attachment was now a mutual love in the Lord. He never felt that the day was complete if his heart had not been lifted up by her prayers as well as his own.

Though her mother scoffed at first, soon she also came to Christ with a younger daughter. Mr. Stocking called Sarah the best theologian among the Nestorians and often said. "If I want to write a good sermon, I first talk with her, and then have her pray for me while I write."

In March it was seen that she must die, still she had a

mission to fulfil, and her Saviour gave her grace to fulfil it. In Persia victory over death had been heard of, but, till then, never witnessed, and Sarah was chosen to show what it is to fall asleep in Jesus. Perhaps the death-bed of no one was ever watched with more eager interest. "Will Christ come and receive us to himself according to his promise?" was a question they stood ready to answer according as He manifested Himself to Sarah. The five months between her conversion and her death were very precious to her friends. She sometimes had long talks with Miss Fiske about Heaven. She seemed to look in on its glories, only when she thought of the perishing, she desired to labor longer for them, if God willed. Her companions could not bear to part with her. About the middle of May it was felt that she must go to her family who lived near. It was a beautiful summer day. When morning prayers were through, her teacher told her, and she replied in a low voice, "I would like to be alone a little before I go." With weary step she sought her familiar closet, but it was occupied and she spent an hour in another, and then was ready to go. She went supported by a schoolmate on either side. Stopping in the court she turned to take a last look of the dear home where she had learned of Jesus, and plucking one of the roses by her side passed out.

She suffered intensely for a few days. She was not even able to lie down, still every day she gathered some women about her to tell them of Jesus. Her teacher often found her with her Bible open, and several round her bed, to whom she was explaining it. Her school-mates also loved to go and pray with her.

One Saturday in June her father was called to preach in Tergawer, twenty-five miles distant. He went to see what Sarah would say. She said, "Go father, and I will pray for you." Sabbath morning came and Sarah was almost home. Miss Fiske once more committed her into the hands of a "very present" Saviour. She had to return to her scholars, first requesting the mother to send for her, when the Master came. In the afternoon, in a paroxysm of suffering, she said "Call my father." They reminded her where he was. "Yes, I remember, let him preach Christ, I can die alone." Then she said "Call Miss Fiske," and her sister rose to go, but Sarah remembered it was the hour for prayer meeting and beckoning to her said, "She is in meeting now, don't call her." Perhaps with that teacher present, she had not so clearly discerned the Lord. Her sufferings were now so great, she could not speak. Then, in a clear voice, she said, "Mother raise me that I may commit my spirit," for she never spoke to Christ save on her knees. She forgot that good word of the Lord, "I will have mercy and not sacrifice." Christ is not pleased when we add to the measure of the suffering that He sends, and still one feels that He is less displeased with our mistakes in that direction, then when they go to the opposite extreme of self indulgence. Held up by those strong arms, as often before, she said, "Lord Jesus receive ——" and there she stopped, prayer had ended, instead of the last word of the earthly prayer was the beginning of the heavenly adoration. While she was speaking Jesus answered. The teacher had just sat down among her pupils when the message came, "Sarah sleeps." She was buried that same evening, (June 13) according to Eastern custom (Acts V. 6 and 10). The whole school followed her to the grave which was near that of Mrs. Grant. The first fruit of the school lies fitly by the side of her who planted that tree in the garden of the Lord. Miss Fiske said, "I am glad that the first to love Christ was the first to be with Him in Heaven and still love to think of her as waiting for those with whom she prayed on earth." Now teacher and scholar are together before the throne of God and of the Lamb.

The case of Hannah also calls for grateful mention. She was the daughter of an intelligent and well-to-do Nestorian, who brought her to the Seminary in 1845. Miss Fiske objected to her youth, but paternal importunity prevailed. As soon as her father turned to leave, she began to scream, but he said she must stay and "learn wisdom." The teacher took her into her lap to soothe her, but her bleeding hands bore the marks of the nails of her new protege for many days. She learned wisdom very slowly. She had her fits of rage so often that she was sent home sometimes for weeks. In the winter of 1850, she began to love the truth, yet still she showed so much self-will, she was often told that if she was indeed a christian, God would subdue that will. She did not see it and thought they were too strict. God rectified the evil in an unusual way. The premises had once been occupied by an Oriental bath, and contained deep pits that had been used to absorb the water. One evening Miss Fiske had forbidden the pupils to do certain things. They assented and went out, and instantly the cry rose "Hannah is in the well," they led the teacher to the place saying "The earth opened and swallowed her up." The covering of one of the pits had given way and she had fallen about twenty feet. Fortunately "there was no water in the pit," and in a few days she was well, but very weak and gentle. Her own account of it was, that when the rest said "We will obey our teacher," she stamped her foot saying, "I did right, and will do it again," and while the words were on her lips she sank into the earth. She did not know what had happened, but felt that God was dealing with her, and lying there bruised and helpless made a solemn vow to God. "Henceforth thy will, not mine." From that time she was a pattern of gentleness. Her father saw the change and said "Hannah knows nothing but God's will. Should she die I would know she was with Christ, she is so like Him." The school learned of her to be Christ-like. She was ready to suffer anything for the sake of doing good. Her father said to her one day, "Badal the son of the herdman wants you to go to the mountains with him, and —— wants you here. It shall be as you say." She chose the privations of the mountain home and went there June 8, 1858. She was happy in her self-denying life for Jesus' sake, but her health sank under her privations, and she visited her old home hoping to be better, but instead she only gave another happy testimony to the blessedness of knowing no will but God's, and then went home. On her dying bed she sent word to Miss Fiske in America. "I love to have God do just as He pleases. I thank you for all your love, and especially for showing me my Saviour." She died December, 1860. It is pleasant to add that in 1861 her brother to whom her inheritance had fallen, gave it all to carry on the work in the mountains to which she had devoted her life.*

Let us turn from these to a very different character, also a fruit of this same tree. In the autumn of 1845, Deacon Guwergis (George) of Tergawer, brought his oldest daughter, then twelve years of age, to the Seminary. He was notoriously and even defiantly dissolute, and Miss Fiske shrank from receiving one from such a family into her flock. Yet as, like her Master, she was sent not to the righteous, but to the lost, she took her in. Still even then, his greed was so shameless, that she was glad when he was gone. He even asked her to dress his daughter in a new suit of clothes,

*Page 89.

that he might carry home the garments she had on, but this she would not do. She hoped that the winter snows would protect her from his dreaded presence. In February he came when many were weeping over their sins, wearing his Kurdish dagger and ammunition belt, and carrying his gun, and she felt that a wolf had indeed entered the fold. He mocked their religious feelings, and set himself like the Great Adversary to hinder the work of the Spirit. She tried to parry his attacks, but she did not need to do it. Her pupils were too deeply convicted of sin to notice him. His own daughter at length begged him to go with her. "Don't you think that I also can pray?" and he repeated over his Syriac form as a wizard mutters his incantation. His child then as one newly awakened to her own guilt and the glory of the power of Christ to save, implored mercy for herself and for him. As she prayed for mercy on him as a sinner, he doubled up his fist to strike her, but as he said afterward, "God held me back."

The native teacher, Murad Khan, then took him to his own room and labored with him till late at night. Sabbath found him not only unimpressed but even more aggressive in his opposition. At noon Miss Fiske went to his room. He occupied the only chair, and did not rise, so she stood and tried to talk, but she might as well have talked to the tempest. She then took his hand and said, "Deacon Guwergis I see you will not let me speak, and I promise you I will never again attempt it, unless you wish it, on this condition; that when we stand together in the great day before God, you will bear witness that on this 22d day of February, 1846, you were faithfully warned of your danger." He did not answer, but in a subdued voice said, "Let me pray." The hand was withdrawn and he went into the next room, whence soon issued a low sound, she could hardly yet believe was prayer. The bell rung and she sent her charge alone to church, while she staid to watch the man whom she feared was only plotting to plunder the premises in their absence. A voice seemed at length to say, "What dost thou here Elijah?" And she took her place with the rest, when the door opened, and he too entered, but how changed. His arms were laid aside. The folds of his large Kurdish turban hung down over his face, and the big tears fell silently through his raised hands. Sinking into the nearest seat, his head rested on the desk. After the benediction Mr. Stocking took him to his study, and there in anguish the late blasphemer cried out, "O my sins:—they are higher than the mountains of Jeloo." "But," said Mr. Stocking, "if the fires of hell were put out would you be troubled?" The strong man bowed down in his agony, crying, "Even if there was no hell, I could not bear this load of sin." That night he could not sleep. In the morning Miss Fiske begged Mr. Stoddard to see him, and soon he came back to tell her that the dreaded Guwergis was sitting at the feet of Jesus. "My great sins," and "my great Saviour" was all he could say. He was gentle as a lamb and humble, and before noon left for home, saying, "I must tell my people of sin and of Jesus." Nothing was heard from him for two weeks when Priest Eshoo found him telling his neighbors "of sin and of Jesus." He had begun family prayer, and at that moment was surrounded by a number weeping for their sins. So changed was he, and his words so earnest, that some thought him insane, but his meekness under insult amazed them, and gave many their first idea of vital piety. Till then, religion to them consisted in the repetition of forms, or in fasting, but the transformation of character by the Spirit of God was to them a new revelation. He brought his family to the city and soon came to see Miss Fiske. As he opened the door, she stood on the opposite side of the room, but the tears stood in his eyes as he reached out his hand, saying "I know you did not believe me, but you will love me, will you not?" and she wondered at her lack of faith. Two of his brothers also sought the Saviour, and his own growth in grace surprised all that knew him. When his daughter came back March 30th, an uncle came with her rejoicing in Christ. Mr. Stocking asked how he had been led into the kingdom and learned that he had promised his brother Guwergis to spend the Sabbath with one of the native teachers of the Seminary, who prayed with him till he threw away his dagger as something for which he had no more use. The native helpers felt that he outstripped them in the heavenly race. In April as many as nine persons in Hakkie, the village of Deacon Guwergis, five of them members of his own family, gave evidence of true piety, and the whole village listened to his preaching. He always loved the Seminary as his spiritual birth place. Once on rising from his knees he exclaimed, "God forgive me, I forgot to pray for the school," and so knelt down again, and it was done in such simplicity and sincerity that it did not call forth even a smile from those that heard it.

After his conversion, the deacon devoted himself to labors in the mountains. One might always see a tear and a smile on his face, as he spoke of sin and Jesus. He traversed the region many times on foot, with his Testament and hymn book in his shepherd's scrip. At the foot of the cliffs he would sing "Rock of Ages," and at the mountain springs "There is a fountain filled with blood." He warned every man night and day with tears that in Jesus was their only hope. He died, March 12, 1856, and, as his mind wandered, spoke continually of "free grace." These were almost his last words. The daughter who prayed with him that first Saturday was with him then, and her prayer the last earthly sound he heard.

It may seem strange that one so notorious for wickedness should be allowed to enter the Seminary, but Oriental ideas of hospitality are very decided and to do good to a people, they must feel that one is their friend. No protection from government can take the place of their loving confidence, and while help was at hand to repel violence if needed, the highest usefulness required that patient love should have its perfect work.

Another instance of the usefulness of the Seminary among the relatives of the pupils must here be mentioned. March 2, 1846, a father called to ask if his daughter was among the converts. Surprised at such a question from a drunkard, he told the story of his own conversion, and his prayers showed him no stranger at the mercy seat. The daughter had given more trouble than any in school, and several times had almost been sent away, but now father and daughter spent the evening together in prayer, and a few days later the mother came and staid till she also came to Christ. She was a sister of Priest Abraham, and had been so clamorous and profane in her opposition, that for years her good brother had dreaded to meet her, but now instead of her blasphemy, he heard her singing the praise of his and her Redeemer.

CHAPTER VIII.

DARK DAYS.

THIS mission has encountered less opposition than others, but it has not been free from trial. June 19th, 1844, the brothers of Mar Shimon issued this order: "Be it known to you all, ye readers at Seir, that if ye come not to us to-morrow we will excommunicate you from our most holy church. Your finger nails shall be torn out. We will hunt you from village to village, and kill you if we can." Miss Fiske was spending the summer there with the Seminary, and it was deemed best to send the pupils home. When told this they wept aloud, and their teachers wept with them. The girls could hardly tear themselves away, and when they did the lament arose: "We shall never hear the Word of God again!" Their teacher gave them up to Christ, trusting that He would bring them back, and others with them. A German Jew said, in his broken English: "In other lands I have seen much bad to missionaries, but nothing bad like this, to take leedle cheeldren from words of Jesus Christ."

Deacon Isaac, a brother of Mar Shimon was ashamed of it. Eight years after he asked leave to speak to the school, and said: "Do all you can to help your teachers, for I once troubled them and it has made my life bitter ever since," and the good man broke down. Then added: "I have vowed to God to help Miss Fiske to the utmost of my power as long as I live," and all who knew him know that he kept his word. When he was first thoughtful, (1849), he heard that a pupil was in the habit of praying *for* him, he insisted on her praying *with* him, and though he had rare force of character, and Sarah of Tiary was more noted for devotion than for mental ability, yet he learned from her in a child-like spirit; another fulfillment of the Word : "A little child shall lead them." He has been occasionally a most acceptable teacher in the Seminary. When Miss Fiske left, in 1858, he promised her to do all in his power for her sex till she came back, and next Sabbath found him teaching a class of women. With us, Governors sometimes teach in the Sabbath School, but in Persia it is a very different thing for a brother of the Patriarch to teach a class of women. Along with unfeigned piety he had more true refinement than most of his countrymen, and few showed kindness with such delicacy.

When the infant daughter of Priest Eshoo—named Sarah, after her sainted sister,—lay dying, Mar Shimon forbade her burial in the cemetery. He had a mob all ready to carry out his will, but she lingered on and disappointed him that day. Next day she died, and the Patriarch had free course. A pious carpenter, however, defied his anathema, and made her coffin. The mission appealed to a former Governor, but Mar Shimon paid no attention to his messages. Miss Fiske wrote : "In our trouble we love to look up at the dear child sweetly resting with her Saviour. May the Sabbath bring us rest." But it found them still in deep waters. The Governor sent to demand the digging of a grave, but the mob would not allow it. It was suggested that a promise from the Priest, not to preach any more, would bring relief. "Never!" was the answer : "Let my dead lie unburied. I will not go back from serving Christ!" The Governor advised to bury in one of the villages. So in the chapel they listened to a sermon from the words "He must through much tribulation enter the Kingdom of God." Then bearing the little coffin and singing the 46th Psalm they passed close by the door of the Patriarch and out of the city gate to the green hill-side, at Seir, where they laid the little one to rest. The Patriarch now commanded to break up the schools, and forbade preaching in the churches. He excommunicated Mar Yohanan and made common cause with the French Lazarists. Deacon Guwergis boldly encountered him in his own house, and avowed his purpose to go on preaching till he died. "See," said Mar Shimon, "how his face shines. If he is so bold before us what will he be in the mountains?" Did he think of Stephen?

Even in the Seminary the pupils were not safe on August 25th a message came that the brother of one was dying and wanted to see her. She was willing to go, but Miss Fiske learned that the brother was well, and that the messenger had come from Mar Shimon's house, who had charged him to hide his purpose from that Satan, Miss Fiske, and if need be, take the girl by force. But the teacher knew how to guard her fold. Three days later, the schoolmaster in Charbash fled, wounded, from the servants of Mar Shimon, to the mission, and his brother followed him, having escaped from similar violence.

Mar Shimon now made common cause with the Persian oppressors of his people. Dawood Khan had been appointed their protector, and Mar Shimon, by promising his aid to Persian efforts against the Khan, secured their co-operation against the mission.

Yahya Khan, Governor of the Province, now aided Mar Shimon to the utmost, and as he was brother-in-law to the Shah, he had great power for evil. But in September the

Shah died, and the power of Yahya Khan perished with his master. Mar Shimon also retired into Turkey and his servants were put under bonds to keep the peace.

A few years later Asker Khan undertook to wear out the saints of the Most High. He caused native helpers to be beaten and fined, and then denied all redress. Encouraged by the Prime Minister, he defied all interference. At one time he issued an order that no school should be opened without his sanction, and that all teachers should report to him. His attitude towards the Seminary appears in the order "Allow no girls in your schools; they are for boys only." But there was a power that said to this flood of wrath, also, "Hitherto shalt thou come, and no further; and here shall thy proud waves be stayed," for Asker Khan fell under Kurdish daggers, and the billows were quiet. Not, however, before much evil had been wrought. Among others, Sanum, the wife of Joseph, suffered in the poisoning of her children, by a neighbor; but, though arsenic was found in the food, though a portion of it caused convulsions and death to the animal that ate it, though no one else had access to it, and a Jewess testified that the guilty party had recently applied to her husband for arsenic, Asker Khan not only refused to investigate but insulted Joseph, beat his aged father, and told the villagers to shoot Joseph if he came again to the village.

A royal order was procured commanding investigation, but the criminals were only detained for a few days, and as they would not confess, Asker Kahn proposed that the mission should intercede for their release, and when they declined to do so, declared that had he known that beforehand, he would not have touched the case, and so dismissed it.

CHAPTER IX.

PRAYERFULNESS OF NESTORIAN CONVERTS.

THIS has been so marked as to call for special notice. In 1846 the prayers in the Boys' Seminary were very remarkable. Some spent several hours a day in prayer, and their language was both intense and scriptural. At one time they beg that the dog may have a crumb from the children's table, again with the publican they smite upon their breasts. Now in the far country they cry for the bread of their Father's house, and again sinking in the waves, they cry, "Lord save, we perish," or they desire to build on the rock of ages though tempests roar and torrents rage around them.

Mr. Stoddard once saw three men riding in the road, their horses went at random, and their heads were bare in the cold March wind. He took them at first for dervishes, but on coming nearer heard the voice of prayer. The eyes of all were closed, and when one stopped, the next went on. He left them undisturbed. He once heard an old man praying in the church by himself in a low tone thus: "Our Father in Heaven—Always going after Satan—O! Lord Jesus Christ—Hallelujah—Forever and ever Amen." The prayer was very broken, but comprehensive. He came to God as his father. He confessed his sin. He cried to Christ as his only helper. He praised God for His mercy and then closed in the usual form.

Mar Ogin of Ishtazin when in great pain, some times used

words like these: "O Lord Jesus, Thou art the King of glory, King of Kings, and Lord of Lords. Thou art great and holy, and merciful. I am a sinner, condemned, my face is black, my bones are rotten. O Lord Jesus, have mercy upon me, poor and blind, and naked and miserable. O Lord Jesus Christ, I am vile, I am lost, but do thou remember me."

In their longing for Christ they would say, "Blessed Saviour we will cling to the skirts of thy garments, and hope for mercy till our hands are cut off." A common petition was, "O Lord never leave us to deny Thee, even the blood of our necks," most expressive words in a land where so many criminals are beheaded. In one village where they brought their offering every Sabbath, some poor women who used to bring eggs, offered this prayer: "O Lord our hens are not laying, please show us some other way by which we can earn our penny." One having occasion to pass through the Seminary, heard as follows: "We hang over a lake of fire with a heavy burden on us, by a single hair, and that almost broken. Again we are in a ship burned almost down to the water, the flames are just seizing on us. O God, have mercy! O Lamb of God have mercy on us."

Is it strange that missionaries thought it a privilege to pray in Syriac when they had such fervent spirits with whom to pray?

The last communion service before Miss Fiske left Persia, occurred in May, 1858, one of the finest of the charming days in Oroomiah at that season. Mr. Stoddard had entered into rest, and his widow with Dr. Perkins and family and Miss Fiske were to sit down with the Nestorian converts at the table of the Lord, for the last time on earth. All who had been connected with the Seminary were to lodge there, so as to gather together the household once more in the old home. As yet none knew that she was going, for she would have nothing turn away their thoughts from Christ. As many as sixty or seventy were present. When all had gathered in the school-room she asked the Master to preside over the meeting, and gave the words "Looking unto Jesus" as the key-note of the occasion. All felt that they sat together in heavenly places in Christ Jesus, and their eyes were opened to the fullness of his words, "There am I in the midst of you." They were invited to speak freely of their joys and sorrows, that together they might lay them all on their burden bearer. The first to speak was Hanee, one of the two brought by Mar Yohanan at the beginning. She had just buried her only child, and holding her arms as though the little one still rested on them, she said: "Sisters, at our last communion you saw my little babe in these arms. It is not here now. I have laid it into the arms of Jesus, and come to tell you of a sweet as well as a bitter in affliction. When the rod is sent, let us not only kiss, but press it to our lips. When I stood by that little open grave I said: The time I have given to my babe I will give to souls, and I try to do it; pray for me." (After the death of her child she used to gather the women in the room where it died, and talk and pray with them.) When she ceased all were in tears. The leader said: "Who will pray!" and Sanum, whose children were poisoned, led in prayer, as few could pray for childless mothers. There was perfect stillness during the prayer, save as the sweet voice of her own babe sometimes added pathos to it. A short pause followed, and to the surprise of all, the voice of Nazloo was heard in another part of the room,—for they had supposed her on her death-bed: "Sisters I have come back from the brink of the grave! May I tell you that it is very different being a christian in this pleasant school room, and being a christian there. Are you sure that you are on the rock Christ Jesus?" One of the early pupils who had come many miles that day, said: "I could think but one thought all the way. 'Freely, ye have received; freely give.' We have certainly received freely. How much have we given. Can we not do something for souls?" They were then asked if they were ready to search for them and lead them to Christ. Many pledged themselves to the work, and to bring the names of those labored with, to the next communion, that all might pray for them; and the first letter Miss Fiske opened in Boston contained the names of those with whom each had prayed and labored. As many as twelve spoke a few words, and more than that number led in prayer during the two hours they were together. After dinner, class prayer meetings were held, and the voice of prayer arose in nearly every room. The chapel bell was unnoticed, and each company had to be summoned separately to church. There Miss Fiske led each to a seat, that they might be together, and seated herself behind them. She counted ninety-three sisters in Christ before her, and recalled the time when she had not one among them all. No wonder she inwardly exclaimed: "What hath God wrought!" There was only one among the ninety-three with whom she had not prayed, and that evening, as she was devising how to bring it about, the Lord sent her unexpectedly to her room, and they also bowed together in prayer. Thirty-nine converts, six of them from the Seminary, were added that day to the communicants.

The day Miss Fiske left Oroomiah, many of her pupils met to bid her good-bye. They asked: "Could we not have one more prayer meeting before you go?" She said she could not lead their devotions then. "You need not," was the answer, "we will carry you to-day." Seventy were soon in her room, which they called "The Bethel." "Blest be the tie that binds," was sung, and six prayers were offered. Esli asked, that when Elijah went up they might all see the chariot and catch the falling mantle, and not sit down to weep, but smite Jordan, and passing over, go to work. She then reminded Christ of his promise not to leave them orphans, (JOHN, 14:8), and begged him not only to come, but to abide with them when their teacher was gone. She asked that in their long land journey the sun might not smite the missionaries, but that he would spread a table for them in the wilderness, and give his angels charge to keep them in their going over the precipitous roads. That when they passed through the rivers, the waters might not overflow them. That the Angel of the Lord might ever encamp round their tents; that on the fire-ship, (steamers from Trebizond to Constantinople, and thence to Smyrna), the flame might not kindle upon them, and when on the winged ship, that He would keep them in the hollow of His hand, and bring them to their desired haven. She then asked that the aged mother of their teacher might be spared to fold her daughter in her arms before she departed in peace. Here she paused, and then added in a more tender tone : "May her dust not mingle with her father's dust, but may she come back to us, till her dust shall mingle with her children's dust, and with them go up to meet the Lord."

One, who before conversion was very obstinate and rude, in writing to Miss Fiske after her return, said : "I remember how you used to put your arms round me and tell me how Christ died, not for friends, but for enemies, like me. I did not understand it then, but now, I cannot sufficiently express my gratitude. I know you are happy with your mother, though your heart is here, and she is happy in the sight of your face; yet these earthly meetings are soon over, but that meeting with the risen Lamb, and with God, our Father, will be more blessed and unending. If separations, too, are so trying now, what must be those of the last day? May I not be separated from you then. We miss you much, but the Teacher who is better than all has taught us this winter. The Lord Jesus has watered us with heavenly rain. We waited for the promise of the Father, and now, when we retire from the school-room, in many parts of the building two girls are found praying together. I have also selected two women to pray for, and some of the women of our village sit at the feet of Jesus."

In 1846 two pupils spent a night alternately praying for their brothers. They felt "We will not let thee go except thou bless us." True, the missionaries insisted on regular hours of sleep. Yet one writes: "Sometimes I have gone to their cold closets to induce them to stop, but the fervor of their prayers has oftener driven me to mine." There were but few closets, and often three or four might be seen waiting their turn. If they only had some of those at home that are seldom entered! The Bible of one was found open at the 51st Psalm, and no part of the large page was free from the marks of tears.

A poor woman came one day weeping for her sins, and sat down on the floor. The teacher was soon at her side, pointing her to Christ. She prayed with her, and asked her to pray. "But I don't know your prayers." "Don't try to pray like anybody else, but just tell God how you feel, and what you want—" "May I say to God just what is in my heart?" When assured that she might, she fell on her face, saying between her sobs, "O, God, I am not fit even to be an old broom to sweep with." This was the most worthless thing the poor woman could think of, and she soon learned that His grace is sufficient for us.

A good man brought his wife to spend a few days in the Seminary. Then he came again to get her, and while he was talking with Miss Fiske, she was passing through the room without seeing him. But he saw her, and reached out his hand. She put her hand in his, and when he asked, "Is Christ become beautiful?" answered, looking up in his face, with a very gentle "I think so," and then they went into the teacher's room to pray together.

In 1846, after a pleasant evening in Geog Tapa, among enquirers, Hanee came and asked Miss Fiske, "Would you like to be alone?" It was the first time a Nestorian had asked her that question, and it thrilled her heart like the first voice of a native woman that she heard in prayer. To use her own words: "I followed the dear child to the best closet she could give me—a manger in which she had spread fresh hay, saying, as she turned to go, 'stay just as long as you like.' It was not her fault if I did not there meet Him, once laid in a manger for us."

At first Miss Fiske prayed alone for her school, but before she left Persia, two-thirds of her pupils had relatives who prayed for their salvation. One morning in 1856, a mother walked three miles through the snow to ask if there was any special religious interest in the school. "Why do you ask?" replied Miss Fiske. "I have been thinking of you continually for two or three days, and last night I dreamed that God was visiting you by his Holy Spirit, so when I woke, I rose and baked, and hurried away. I was so anxious about my daughter; can I see her?" When she was told that her daughter was among the enquirers the night before, she sank down where she stood, weeping for joy. The heart of the teacher grew strong, feeling that the mothers were praying with her. This one went to another room to see her daughter, and a missionary could not restrain his tears as he listened to her earnest prayer, saying: "This is more to me than anything I have seen in Persia." A father once wrote: "Yesterday I invited some friends to my house, and we prayed for the school, and while praying for you, we felt our own sins very much, and cried to God to save us from their power." Nor were the pupils lacking in interest for their friends who were out of Christ. During the summer vacation in 1850 Hanee, who used to spend several hours a day praying for her mother, so pressed her to come to Christ, that one day she answered roughly: "Stop your praying and weeping for me; you will cry yourself blind." "O, mother," was the answer, "I would gladly become blind, if thereby you might be brought to Jesus."

The members of the Seminary were specially interested in the monthly concert. On that Monday they wanted two or three meetings, and in 1846 it was hard to induce them to study. The voice of intercession for the world was heard all day long, now all together, now in little companies of five or six, and again each alone, they pressed the same request.

In April, not satisfied with an extra meeting, they were induced to close it near sunset, only by the promise of another like meeting next day. They wrote to Mt. Holyoke Seminary: "The monthly concert is a very sweet day to us, we love no other so well except the Sabbath."

In January, 1849, they were very earnest in prayer, mostly for themselves, as unfit to pray for others. Up to the 29th only two or three of the unconverted showed any interest, but that night many were so distressed for their sins, they could not retire to rest. Christians were praying for others without hope, and many of these last were crying for mercy. One began, "O, Lord, throw us a rope, for we are out in the sea on a single plank, and wave after wave is dashing over us," and their whole spirit and manner corresponded to their strong figurative language.

The work extended to the villages. From Degala, Deacon Joseph wrote that even young children heard their parents pray so much, that they also did the same. The women also met frequently by themselves. "One day I led some men to a place, where they could hear women praying within the house, and they begged me to teach them also how to come to God."

Among a people so excitable, the missionaries avoided appeals to the emotions, though the conscientious lives of those who prayed, showed that they were sincere.

On the evening of the second Sabbath in Jan., 1850, Miss Fiske did not feel well, and remained in her room alone. The door opened gently, after the prayer meeting was over, and a little group passed through very quietly. She rose to follow, when she heard several in earnest prayer. She turned to the stairs, and there the same sound came up from many closets. What did it mean? There had been nothing unusual in the meeting, and she felt that it was from above. It was late before all retired, and they resumed the same employment in the early morning. That week domestic duties were performed earlier than usual, and thoroughly, and then they hurried to their closets, in which some spent five hours each day of the week. Saturday afternoon was devoted by several to prayer for a blessing on the morrow, and a blessed Sabbath ensued. In the morning service all were very tender. At dinner many seats were empty. No voice was heard that day but that of prayer. Miss Fiske never knew such a Sabbath, neither before nor since. In the afternoon the feeling was overpowering. There was no request for prayer, but unbroken silence and the perfect performance of every duty, without a word spoken. Some asked to be excused from supper, but at length all were seated at the table. The blessing was asked, and the steward began to help them, but no plate was touched, for even the uninterested gazed in wonder. Their teacher said: "I am just as sure that the Lord would have you eat as that He would have you pray, and I beg you to eat in order to have strength to pray." This argument had power, and they silently withdrew to make the most of their renovated strength.

For two months each day proved that these prayers were heard. There was less excitement but no loss of interest, to the close of the term. The sustained prayerfulness of those months surprised their teachers. Prayer was the latest sound of the evening, the watchword of midnight, and the lark song of the dawn. One girl, nine years of age, would retire only when allowed to rise and pray, if she awoke through the night, and about 3 o'clock every morning, her earnest petitions awoke her teachers.

The hours of social prayer were full of tenderness. They seemed to press close to the Mercy Seat. The school, their parents and friends were all lovingly remembered. The hour always seemed too short, and though of varied character, always of thrilling interest. One moment they professed an overwhelming sense of sin, as committed against a Holy God, and the next offered a petition that the Holy One would look on Golgotha and bid them live. Again the sense of manifold sin prompts the cry: "But we fear our sins have covered Golgotha out of sight! Oh, lift not the Mercy Seat from off the Holy Ark, to look on the law we have broken; but look into the grave of Jesus and bid us live!"

Their labors for their unconverted schoolmates, and for visitors, were full of Christ. The hour after supper was usually spent in personal labor from room to room, and the sounds then heard on all sides made it delightful to be in a strange land for Jesus' sake. Their teacher desired more silent devotion, but Mr. Stoddard feared to have it checked, lest the spirit of prayer should be lost through the interference, and some things looked that way. There was one who spent hours daily in her closet, but her teacher heard all she said. So at a fitting opportunity, in a very gentle way, she suggested a change. "I will try to pray more quietly, but I never thought that I was heard." That night her voice was not heard, but her prayer was very short, and after midnight the teacher was awakened by the voice of prayer on the flat earthen roof. She stepped out quietly, and there was the suppliant wrapped in a blanket thanking God for a place to pray in. She had no heart to interfere further, and Mr. Stoddard was much amused at her success. In another case, fearing for the health of her pupil, she led the physician to the outside of the door, but neither did he venture to interrupt such communion with God.

Three days in the week meetings were held with women and were well attended. The older pupils went that they might learn evangelistic work, and both their prayers and modest counsels were appropriate and to edification.

Several, at this time, were hopefully converted, among them a girl whose mother had suffered much for Christ. Often, on returning from evening meeting, has that mother been kept out an hour in a piercing winter wind, and been beaten besides, but she never denied her Lord. Her friends said that the conversion of her child was the answer to her prayers and faithful endurance.

At the close of the term a prayer meeting in each room continued till the last moment. Even those without hope clung to the others and begged for their prayers.

There is one connection of this work with prayer that must not be overlooked, and that is the connection with the prayers offered in a distant land. While those two enquirers on that first Monday of 1846 were making closets among the wood in the cellar, it is distinctly remembered by some, that Mary Lyon said that morning "We must pray more for Miss Fiske and her school." Her words were heeded, and the answer noted when they heard of what took place in Persia that day. Almost the same things might be said of the same day in 1847 and 1849. The revival of 1856 began unexpectedly, but, when on the night of February 17, that pupil could not sleep because the whole school lay on her heart, and at midnight sought the help of her teacher in intercession, letters from America showed that they were not wrestling alone. In the first week of February, 1859, meetings were held every evening in Mt. Holyoke Seminary, to pray for the school in Oroomiah. Miss Fiske was then in South Hadley, and a letter from Miss Rice written that week says, "God is with us, souls are seeking Christ, and I am so strengthened for labor that I am sure Christians are praying for us more than they did last month."

The monthly concert of prayer for missions is not the unmeaning form, or the barren service that some think it is. Well does a missionary say: "I have so often felt that I was reaping in answer to the prayers of those at home, that my heart is full, and my first and last word is 'Pray for us.'"

The review of monthly concerts in heaven will make some startling revelations, little looked for even by some of their regular attendants.

CHAPTER X.

THE MOUNTAIN NESTORIANS.

IT is impossible to give a history of the mountaineers or of missionary work among them. We can only give some hints of the connection between them and the Seminary. As the Seminary could not enter the mountains, God brought the mountains to it. The massacre of 1843 sent fugitives to the plains both East and West of their devastated homes. Near the close of the year a wretched group came asking for "the lady who teaches Nestorian girls." She saw three before her and replied: "Silver and gold we have not, but we will give you a home for these." This was not what they wanted, but while the parents debated the matter under the tall sycamores, the little ones, quick to respond to kindness, staid with the stranger. By and by the father and mother gave them leave to stay till they returned to Tiary, and the announcement called forth a very tender "thank you" from the girls. They were taken in, washed, clothed and fed, and though at first they knew neither the alphabet nor good manners, they made good progress in both. Better still, Sarah and Nazee were among the converts of 1846, and Heleneh was among those of 1848.

The last days of the spring term, 1849, were full of interest. The teachers did not understand it then, but now they see that God was preparing his first witnesses for their work in that difficult field. Sarah had long been known as "the praying Sarah," her mind was not so gitted as some, but she prayed with all prayer and supplication in the spirit as Deacon Isaac could testify. At this time the prospect of vacation instead of diverting from prayer, only produced more intense earnestness. Some of the older pupils were unwilling to go away till they had prayed with each one in the school alone. On the last morning they separated in a very prayerful spirit. The quiet of the hour seemed heavenly. Not a loud voice, heavy step, or slamming door was heard, all was sacredly still. The lambs were sent out from the fold with peculiar anxiety.

Some were to go into families where they would find no christian fellowship, but much and bitter opposition; others to villages equally destitute of Christian sympathy; and as they went forth the prayer arose from full hearts, that God himself would be to them a sanctuary for a little while in the places where they went. But while their thoughts were on those belonging to the plain, God had in view those who were going forth to years of separation or even life-long exclusion from the means of grace.

That evening, after the rest had gone, Miss Fiske heard intercession for the absent ones as late as ten o'clock, and fearing for the health of the suppliant, she went to advise her to retire; but as she listened to her strong crying for each of the school by name, she could not disturb her. Sarah, though her teacher did not know it, was even then suffering. Next day she was worse, and for a week was dangerously sick. She felt disappointed at first, when she found God was calling her back to health, but said: "Thy will, not mine, be done."

April came and a scarcity in the plains drove the fugitives back to their mountain home. It was hoped the children might remain, but the parents were only too glad to get their daughters away from influences they abhorred. It was hard for the children to go. It was no less hard for their friends to think of these lambs as at the mercy of wild beasts, far from human help. Even if they died, years might elapse before the fact could be known in Oroomiah, and so communion with God was the only source of comfort. When they left, the whole school came together for the parting prayer. The three went to bid farewell to their closets, and only He who seeth in secret knows how they prayed. After a few scripture words of comfort the teachers commended them to God. Then a pupil proposed that all who would pledge themselves to remember them in every prayer, should join hands around them and give their pledge to God. About twenty thus continued in prayer till the last moment, and as the three passed out, they could speak but one word, "The pledge." For years after, every prayer in the seminary asked for blessings on "our sisters in Tiary."

Her teacher had often seen the large quarto page of Sarah's Testament wet with her tears. After she left she found the whitewash of her closet wall marked in the same way. She did not mention it, lest undue sacredness should attach to the place, and yet she would not obliterate marks so full of comfort to her own heart. Sarah had gone but a little way before she begged leave to retire a little from the road to pray. And so weeping and praying they went into a den of lions. We shall see persecution beating pitilessly on them, like their own mountain storms, but we shall also see the Hearer of prayer preserving them unharmed; and if we hear less from Sarah, it may be because the things to be known about her will be heard more peacefully in that place where the faithful unto death receive the crown of life.

Nothing was heard from them till October, 1850, when

Yonan and Khamis went to seek them. They spent a Sabbath in the house of Nazee, but she was from home. They write. "We preached thrice to large congregations. They brought us her Testament to preach from, and as the result of her teachings, we find them excelling other places in knowledge of the Gospel. Monday she came about noon, and how can we describe the joy of that meeting? Most of the following night was spent in sweet Christian communion with her. We wondered at the respect shown her. We longed to pray with her, but custom here forbade it. When we bade her goodbye she said, 'Here is my love for my teachers, my schoolmates, and all that know me. Tell them to pray that God would keep me in this place of temptation.'—We cannot read that unmoved. She asks neither for exemption from trial nor comfort in it, but for victory over it.—'We left her looking after us till we were out of sight, and wiping away her tears." They say somewhat the same of Heleneh, but Sarah they did not see. She was in another village, and her husband, whom she had been forced to marry, would not allow her to see them.

Mr. Coan visited Tiary in August, 1851. He crossed the Zab at Chumba on two long poplar trees, and Nazee stood on the bank to welcome him; then while she went to prepare a place the Malik took him to his house. Disappointed, she followed to treasure up every word and staid to converse on spiritual things until near midnight. She is persecuted by her own mother and ungodly neighbors, for she is a shining light. Some friends in America sent her clothing, but her neighbors tore it in pieces before her. She only prayed for them. She expected fresh insults because of this visit, but prayed that nothing might separate her from the love of Christ. Long before day she sought Mr. Coan again to converse on the things of Christ, her eyes filled with tears. When they parted at the river-side, he pointed her to the words, "Come unto me all ye that labor and are heavy laden," and in broken accents commended her to Him that uttered them.

In September, 1861, Yonan again visited the mountains, and in a village of Tiary, where some two thousand were eating, drinking and carousing, Heleneh recognized him at once. They talked from morning till near sunset, and though they might not go alone to pray, yet in sight of the crowd they approached the mercy seat. The spectators little dreamed to whom they were speaking.

Nazee they found two days after; a widow with two children. She was poor; her house had been burned, but her Testament was saved. She gave them a letter which she had carried about for ten years, waiting for an opportunity to send it. Next day brought them to the home of Sarah, and though she had to leave that night for a distant village, they were able to pray together, and Yonan was happy to find that she too retained the love of Christ in her heart.

The following are extracts from Nazee's letter to friends in Middlebury, Vermont, which she had retained so long: "Know that more than two years ago I left the seminary. I did not wish to leave, for I had learned very imperfectly what the Gospel teaches about our Lord Jesus Christ; but my mother was not willing that I should stay. Dear sisters. when I take your letter in my hands, I long to fly and behold your faces in the body, but the will of the Lord, not mine, be done. When I look within and see no place worthy to thank God for His great grace, I liken myself to the slothful servant; yet though I have not done the will of my Savior, I hope in him that I shall serve him as long as I live. Though we are unworthy we should increase our diligent efforts and prayers that the kingdom of God may come, and His will be done on earth as it is done in Heaven. Beloved sisters, I am not worthy to thank you, and still less to thank God who has led you to show me such kindness, yet greatly do I thank you. I have one request to make; that every time you bow to the God and Father of our Lord Jesus Christ, you will pray for me, for I am in want of all things. Remember also my mother and all my friends. From your unworthy and sinful sister, Nazee, of Tiary."

Mrs. Labaree in her report of work for women in Oroomiah made in October, 1885, says: "Thirty-six years ago Nazee of Tiary, had been taught a short time in the seminary and now we hear of her holding firmly to her faith in Christ though surrounded by darkness which may be felt, and with no human sympathy. Through all these years she has braved the ridicule of rough men who scoff at a woman who can read. Taking her Bible with her to the sheep-folds she allows no day to pass without reading it. She has taught her daughter to read and has tried to teach others. Even her enemies bear witness to her gentle spirit."

In a letter dated April 1, 1887, she writes: "Nazee is a simple-minded warm-hearted old woman, who has kept her faith, rather, who has been kept by the power of God under the most adverse circumstances. Seven or eight years ago she unexpectedly appeared in Oroomiah and staid several months that she might renew her acquaintance with spiritual things. We all felt that in doing for her, we were giving a cup of cold water to one of Jesus Christ's little ones. Of Heleneh and Sarah I know nothing. One of them I think is dead." This last sentence throws a vivid light on the inaccessible seclusion of those mountain homes, and magnifies the grace that has kept weak, helpless women, steadfast amid the merciless hate of cruel men, protracted through so many years.

Mrs. Labaree, in the report already quoted, gives some additional glimpses of the state of things there. She says: "At the last meeting (1884) in Seir, Kemat, wife of Werda gave a report of her two years' work in Tiary, and her simple statements of the degradation of the mountain women greatly touched her hearers. The ignorance and superstition of the people almost defies description. The men often say that woman has no part in the resurrection, and the women themselves have no knowledge of a future life. With the greatest surprise they heard about God, and the story of Christ seemed so wonderful to them, that they could not believe it, especially that he should care for them, and be their Saviour. At first they only listened to mock, but some now come to her and ask to hear again about that wonderful Saviour. Their only idea of religion is to merit heaven by the strict observance of fasts, and they were so horrified by her non-observance of them, that they tried to drive her and her husband away, lest God should punish the whole village for such sacrilege! They were bitterly persecuted, and their lives threatened. The power of a holy life is seen in the respect now shown them, and in the increasing readiness to hear them. She has a strong attachment for her new home and work, and does not think its hardships and privations worth the mention. They have gone back to Tiary, and with them another graduate of the seminary, recently married to a mountain helper. Misky from Bass, has also graduated, and returned to her home this summer.

Even as far back as 1858, at the June monthly concert

four graduates were present with their husbands on their way to the mountains. Guly, wife of Yohanan, who had already spent one year in Little Jeloo. Nargis, wife of Khamis who had spent the winter alone near Amadia was now going with him to Gawar. Hannah was going with Badal to the same district and Eneya the wife of Shlemon his associate "was expecting to leave in a few days."

Guly wrote the following account of her conversion to Miss Fiske: "The first four weeks of the revival I did not realize that I was lost but afterwards my sins were round about me like dark clouds. One night I went to Miss Rice to get her to pray with me. I did not know how to find Christ. She told me, but all that night I saw no light. I was almost in despair. In the morning the sun rose pleasantly, but it was night to me, for I had no portion in God. I could not read in my class, but went to my room resolved not to leave it till I had some token that Christ was mine. I brought nothing in my hands but my sins, which were like mountains. I remembered that word, 'Though your sins be as scarlet, they shall be as white as snow,' and felt that God alone could forgive me. With earnest longing I laid my soul into the hands of Jesus. I heartily engaged to serve him all my life, and in prayer I sought his help. Then I saw light, as though he were present, and I did not wish to rise from my knees, so blessed was that communion. Since then I hope, but sometimes fear I may be deceived. Yet, daily, Christ is more precious, and though old Adam is not dead, yet in the strength of God I will resist him. My dear mother in Christ, my desire is to please God and live for Him, and not for myself. I cannot say that I shall never sin, for I am weak, and my foe is strong, but I seek help from Him who himself was tempted, and can succor me."

Besides those already mentioned. Oshana and Sarah have labored in Amadia. This Sarah is daughter of Priest Abraham of Geog Tapa, and was one of the earliest pupils of the seminary. She was hopefully converted in 1846. In 1849 her father was sent to labor in Ardeshai, one of the most wicked villages of the plain. Great opposition was made by the village to his coming, and his own wife did much to hinder his going, but Sarah did all in her power to encourage him, and it was a letter from her that decided him to go. She spent all her vacations there helping him, and after she graduated in 1850, besides a day school there, she had a Bible class on the Sabbath with the women, and on Friday sent out her pupils to gather them to a meeting in the evening. She thus led several to Christ. Her labors were very systematic. She conversed with one scholar every day, and was noted for her tact and success. Others might act from impulse and soon tire, but her activity was from principle and therefore enduring. Faithful in admonition, she was also noted for gentleness. She wrote to Miss Fiske, "Away from my Christian friends I am sometimes sad, but I am not greater than Him who left heaven to come to earth, and I am grateful for a corner where I may serve so good a master. Come and spend the Sabbath with me if you can. If not, pray much and often for these poor women. Forty or fifty of them come to meeting, and twenty-two receive the truth." She was in the habit of studying the Bible with her father. Notice how she asks prayer not for her own comfort, but for these poor women.

A letter to Miss Fiske, in 1859, gives a good idea of her spirit. "Beloved the good news of revivals in your land, rouses us to warmer zeal. Shall we not also prepare the way of the Lord? We know from the blessings here this winter that Christians with you are praying for us, for the work of the Lord advances, both on the plain and in the mountains. Here in Seir the women say: "Though we have had revivals before, yet never have the words of God had such effect." Mrs. Cochran and I have good meetings with them. I am very happy in laboring for them one by one. A part of them are covenanting to be the Lord's. We ask the Lord to strengthen them to keep that covenant, and entreat you to unite your prayers with ours."

In May she visited Tehoma and thus describes the journey: "Through the favor of our Heavenly Father, I have entered these mountains rejoicing to labor for my people. I am happy that my father and friends favored my coming. Every step of the way my heart has been led to praise my God and thank my teachers, who brought me, so weak and unworthy, to labor amid these desolations. All the way, your counsels have been of great benefit to me. You will be glad to know that the door here is wide open; pray the Lord of the harvest to send forth laborers.

We left Oroomiah, May 6; reached Memikan on the 8th, and stayed three days. On our first Sabbath I met the women.—Sarah was here again in 1885 and found many open doors.—May 12 we went up to the tops of the snowy mountains of Gawar. The cold obliged us to wrap our faces as in January. On the other side we found it warmer, and spent the night at Boobawa, where Yohanan and Guly live. They were absent laboring in Khananis. Only a few came to preaching. The people are very wild and hard. They said: "Yohanan preaches and we revile." May 13 men lay in wait and plundered us after we had crossed the river, but afterwards, of their own accord, restored our property. The sight of this wonderful, fearful river, and the mountains clad with forests, reminded us of Mr. Rhea and his hymn, "Valley of Ishtazin." The thought that you had trodden these frightful precipices greatly encouraged me. At night we reached Jeloo and spent the night in Zeer, which lies in a valley made beautiful by forests, with a river flowing through. The people showed us great hospitality, and were eager to receive the word. On the 14th we left for Bass and spent the Sabbath in Nerik. I shall always remember it with joy, for all the time we were there we were never alone, so many came to hear the word. They said: "What shall we do? We have none to teach us." Half an hour from Nerik we came to Urwintoos. The aunt of Oshana made us her guests. As soon as we sat down the house was filled. They brought a Testament and begged us to read. My heart was glad when I saw how eagerly they listened to the Gospel. After the men had gone the women came to me as those that thirst for water, and I read and conversed with them also. There are many sad deeds of wickedness done here. We reached Tehoma May 17, and I trust that as long as I am here I shall labor for that Master who wearied himself for me.

She returned to Oroomiah in 1860 and left again in 1861 for Amadia, and when she went away, told Mrs. Breath that Miss Fiske had said, when she saw her oldest child for the first time, "Now, Sarah, you will not seek for this child a pleasant home on the plain, like Lot, but rather to do God's will, and then He will give you all things." She hardly needed to add: "I have never forgotten her words, and am not willing to seek my own pleasure by staying here." During the winter of '61-'62 no news came from Sarah, but in March she wrote to Miss Rice: "I did greatly long for the coming of your messenger, and now I thank Him, in whose hands are all things, that he has made us happy by the arrival of letters. Many thanks to you and your dear pupils. The Lord bless them and prepare them for such a blessed work as ours. Our hearts have been contented and happy in seeing some of our neighbors receiving with joy the words of life. Every Sabbath we have a congregation of thirty-five, both men and women, and the number increases. The people here sit in misery and ignorance. They need our prayers and our help. I verily believe that if we labor faithfully—and God help us thus to labor—we shall soon see our church revived and adorned as a bride for Christ. Soon shall these mountains witness scenes that shall make angels glad. Let us pray for these times and labor with Christ for their coming. In the summer her little son died, and she herself was dangerously sick, but she still lives and Mrs. Labaree writes: "There is no woman in the nation more respected for her intelligence, godliness and deep spirituality. It is fitting to add that Miss Fiske's words concerning her children have been fulfilled, in the fact that one of her daughters is now the wife of Rev. J. Wright, missionary at Salmas.

The joyful anticipations of Sarah are endorsed by accounts of a conference of mountain helpers, held in Gawar, in the summer of 1862. At each session, carefully prepared papers were read on practical topics, followed by discussion. One was "Hindrances to our mountain work," such as their ruggedness, deep snows, superstition and persecution. "For rough roads," said Deacon Tamo, "we have goats' hair sandals; for deep snow, snowshoes; for superstition we have the light of the Truth and the sword of the Spirit: and for persecution we have God's promise of divine care." "The duty of faithful pastors," and 'Means for increasing laborers," were among the topics. They engaged to observe the monthly concert and take up collections for the support of a laborer in the mountains, and at the meeting on Sabbath evening the large sum, for them, of fifty-two dollars, was contributed. Among the offerings were a horse, an ox, a sheep and a goat, besides jewelry. From such meetings, held in such a spirit, we may expect large results.

That was twenty-five years ago. Let us look at some of the little centres of light now shining. Selby, one of Miss Fiske's first class, lives at Marbeeshoo, now widowed and grey-haired. In that mountain village, she and Esli, another graduate of the school, have had everything to contend with. When Selby first went there she was the only reader. Now there are nine of her relatives who read, besides others, most of them taught by her. Formerly none would listen when she read to them the Bible. Now, as she goes from house to house, from ten to thirty women come to hear, and often fathers and brothers sit down quietly among them. She is not employed by the mission, and has many family cares, and yet she labors thus steadfastly for the good of her people, overcoming opposition by the persistence of her Christian love. Her son was in college in 1886, and his gentle, yet manly ways, and love of holy Scripture, showed the effects of his mother's training. Esli, who offered that prayer for her departing teacher, has probably no equal for self-denying zeal and persevering effort. Brought up amid the comforts of Oroomiah, and once a teacher in the seminary, she counts it a privilege to spend years in benighted Tergawer, among those constantly liable to be plundered by lawless Kurds, and often goes to other villages to speak to the women, and it should here be stated, that it requires as much self-denial for a native of Oroomiah to go to the mountains as for an American to go to Persia. It must have been a Christ-like spirit that led these two women to tear themselves away from the jubilee meeting in Oroomiah, and hurry back to their dark homes and their work for Christ, but their Saviour does not wait for our slow prayers to fulfil to them his promise, "Lo I am with you always." God bless them.

In 1885, men from the vicinity of Van, told of a woman unlike all others, who read the Bible and lived a most consistent life, but who was always weeping over the gross darkness and bitter hostility of those around her. In the spring of 1886, some of the mission visited the degraded village in which she lived, and found Nazloo, who had gone out from the seminary more than twenty years before, and had long been lost sight of. She called on them with her husband, whom she had brought to Christ. They had gathered a school in their own house, and with a single copy of the Bible, and two or three other books, had taught the scholars to read, and even to some who came from a distance, out of their own limited means, they gave a home. Who can measure the good done by this one woman, far away from all Christian fellowship, and what limit can we put to the usefulness of Christian schools that send forth such light into the darkness? Surely there is more vitality in Christian life than many think there is.

Rabi Rachel also spent a month, in the fall of 1885, among some of the villages of Tergawer, and again in the spring of 1886. She found much to encourage her, notwithstanding the constant terror in which the people live from the Kurds. No wonder she looked worn and haggard after a month's campaign in this difficult field.

We can trace the effects of the teaching of the seminary even to distant lands. Moressa, wife of Priest Yakob accompanied her husband to England a few years ago, where she made a very pleasant impression among the best classes of Christian society by the brightness of her intellect, her lady-like manners, and intelligence in spiritual things. At home she has now much intercourse with Mohammedan women. Hoimar, also another Nestorian woman, has been abroad twice. The last time she came to our own country, and was for several years an assistant at the Chinese Home, in San Francisco. She so won the confidence and esteem of Christian ladies there that they furnished her the means for her return to Persia, where she is now exerting an excellent influence among the women of her own people. Her sister Rachel aided Miss C. Van Duzee, in 1886, in her school at Oola.

CHAPTER XI.
CONCLUSION.

The pupils were early trained to habits of self-denial for the good of others. In 1844 the day scholars made fifty garments for poor children. Next year the question was asked, when some mountaineers came begging for their children, "Who will give her own dress and wear a poorer one till she can make another?" and many responded at once, and so eagerly that she was counted the happiest who gave her best dress. In December, 1848, the monthly concert collection for the mountains was 32 krans ($6.40). They used to devote several hours a week to sewing for some benevolent object. One term the articles thus made were sold for $16.00 and the money sent to Aintab, Turkey.

In 1852, at Geog Tapa, Deacon John preached at the Jan. concert and a few krans were given. At the February concert Deacon Yonan, who had read American prize essays on Beneficence with Miss Fiske spoke to a crowded church on the subject of missions, and then the people were made to read for themselves what the Bible said on the antiquity of benevolent contributions, their being given by the poor as well as the rich, and the blessing God promised to the benevolent. Many spoke in approval of the object and as many as two hundred came together in the afternoon and a contribution of 15 krans followed, one sick boy rising from his bed to deposit his little offering. Saints' days were devoted by many to collecting money for the spread of the Gospel. At the March concert Mr. Stoddard showed them some idols from India and the collection was 25 krans. After this a basket used to be passed around with the box to receive the eggs that were brought by those who had no money. Silver crosses were sometimes found among the coins.

One woman came to ask a missionary lady to pray that she might become a Christian, and when alone gave the only gold ornaments she owned for missions. only. she said, no one must know it. The gold sold for $4.50, and the donor, we need hardly add, became a Christian. Often buttons made from silver coins were cut off from their dresses and put into the contribution boxes.

The most noted revival of benevolence occurred in April, 1861, and was described by Deacon Yonan in a letter to Miss Fiske and Mrs. Stoddard. This is the substance of it: "My heart was never so enlarged before as in the first week of January, which was set apart for universal intercession for the gift of the Spirit. It seemed as if Persia and the whole world was under the power of prayer. When the missionaries met for that purpose, I said: "They are praying for us while we are idle," and it was proposed to devote half an hour each day to prayer. On the last Sabbath in March we went to Geog Tapa, and John gave notice of a collection for missions in India. He said our poverty came in part from our sloth. If we had more zeal we might support a laborer in the mountains at a cost of 20 tomans. I said, "We will support one preacher there, two schools among ourselves, and send what is over to a distance." All fell in with the idea. One cried at once, "I will give one toman, another two monats (a monat is 75 cents). The malik gave a gold imperial ($4.50). I then said, "I am a debtor, write me down 3 tomans." So it went on and though there had been a scarcity for seven years, so that wheat was six times its former price, that was forgotten. One woman gave a head-dress, another her ear-rings and another a silver ornament. A widow proposed to sell her dead husband's coat and give half the price. Another said I have nothing now to offer, but I will give of my work this winter ten yards of cotton cloth. One man not used to coming to church, gave the fruit and prunings (fuel) of fifteen rows in his vineyard. My mother-in-law promised one hundred and twenty-eight pounds of raisins. My uncle and his wife promised a load of wheat (five bushels).

Next day we came into the city. After Mr. Coan had addressed the meeting, Deacon John described the scenes of the day before and showed some of the gifts. Moses said, "It is no disgrace for a sick man not to walk, but if he recovers and still lies in bed, all reproach him. We have grown fat, how long shall we lie under the quilts?" Priest Yakob added, "For twenty-five years we have said, 'let the Lord go before, now that he has come let us give;'" and he gave 2 tomans, so did others. The wife of Mar Yohanan gave a toman of ornaments; her husband gave thirty tomans; Isras, of Degala, gave fifteen tomans and a new vineyard; Sagoo, of Gulpashan, gave his sister Hannah's inheritance, thirty tomans, that had become his at her death.* One who owned only two or three sheep, promised one of them. My little girl, Sherin, gave the new dress she had asked for a few days before, but which had not yet been made. At the evening meeting one gave a gun. There were tithes and sixths, fifths and quarters, thirds and halves of crops. One who had previously given one-fourth of his vineyard now gave one-half. A widow who owned nothing but a cow, pledged four pounds of butter. In Geog Tapa, beside the tithes, seventy tomans were collected, and in Oroomiah two hundred and fifty

* p. 51

tomans. I stood amazed; the glorious God has gone before us in mercy. It is the beginning of a great work for future generations. Heaven rejoices with the joy of blessed Mr. Stocking and Mr. Stoddard in this work of grace. I never knew our people before, and if all were Christians what might we not see?

The marriage of Mar Yohanan in 1859 was a great step in the elevation of women, for marriage had been counted something too unholy for a bishop, and this involved the degradation of the sex. The entrance of the Gospel corrected the error, and that act of the bishop only voiced the general conviction that marriage is to be had in honor among all, even the holiest servants of the church, inasmuch as it nurtures some of the loveliest graces of the Ghristian character. The event caused a stir for a time among those hostile to the truth; but it soon subsided, and the old error that caused it is passing away with the social degradation in which it had its origin.

About the same time Yohanan was ordained to the work of the ministry, without the wearisome ceremonies that had taken the place of the simple forms of the New Testament, the venerable Mar Elias uniting with the missionaries in the laying on of hands; and soon six more, who had only been waiting for some one to lead the way, followed his example. Among them Oshana, Deacon John and Deacon Yakob.

In 1858 the people of Memikan ceased to keep the fasts, because they contradicted free grace through Jesus Christ. Once this would have involved ecclesiastical penalties, and their village would have been destroyed, now it was scarcely noticed. Not that men did not see the trend of the movement, but seeing it they let it have free course.

In Turkey, missionaries have been forced, by persecution,

to form churches to shelter converts driven from their ancient fold; but in Persia that need did not exist; still spiritual minds longed for a more spiritual worship. They had never been present at the Lord's Supper, as observed by the mission, till in the spring of 1854. Some who had been reading an English book on the subject, asked permission to attend, and a few of those who were deemed best prepared for it, were invited to partake. In September of that year, in the large room of the seminary, eleven Nestorians, three of them its graduates, sat down with the missionaries at the Lord's Table. After the service some of them went up stairs and sat down in silence. Miss Fiske, fearing lest the simplicity of our form had given offence, avoided the subject till one asked: "Is it always so when you commune?" "Why, did you not enjoy it?" "Not enjoy it! Christ himself seemed present, presiding at the table. It must have been just so when the disciples met in that upper room, and the question haunted me, shall one of us go out, like Judas, and betray the Lord?" Those most accustomed to mediæval forms, when taught of the Spirit, enjoy them the least, and the more spiritual they become the more they relish simple forms, because instead of attracting attention to themselves they allow the heart to rest in Christ alone. In January, 1855, seventy were admitted after careful examination, and each communion season that year there was an accession of from twelve to thirty. Even in mid-winter some made long journeys and crossed bleak mountains to attend. Hoimar traveled sixty miles through deep snow and bitter cold to be present in January, 1858.

In June that year, all entered into covenant with God previous to the ordinance. The whole number received then was two hundred and forty-nine. At the close of 1861 it was five hundred. The year before it had been observed in every village where there were enough of communicants to call for it. Soon after they adopted a creed and directory for worship, and now the converts have all church privileges, without any violent disruption of old ties.

During the twenty-five years that have elapsed since the writing of "Woman and her Saviour in Persia," the following women mentioned in its pages have finished their earthly course: Sanum, wife of Deacon Joseph, p. 50; Hanee, wife of Deacon Eshoo, p. 52; Martha, p. 67; Eneya, p. 126; Guly, p. 205; Nergis, wife of Priest Khamis, p. 205; Hannah, p. 205; Nergis, wife of the Malik, of Geog Tapa, p. 234; and Munny, pp. 267-269. Most of them died years ago, but Eneya, in 1886, and Martha last winter. Mrs. Labaree says: "They were all good women, and several of them were more than usually consistent and consecrated. Guly, Hannah and Sanum spent a part, and Eneya and Nergis, wife of Khamis, the whole of their married lives, in the mountains, where their husbands were helpers. Hanee accompanied her husband to Tabriz, where he was preacher and Bible agent. Martha taught in the seminary till her marriage. Among them all was none more earnest and devoted than Munny. Her labors for women were abundant. Eight of these graduates married native helpers, and at least seven have had daughters in the seminary.

The jubilee or semi-centennial anniversary of the mission was observed at Oroomiah, July 15 and 16, 1885. More than half of the fifteen hundred who attended the services were women, and they formed the most quiet and attentive part of the audience. Their neat appearance and orderly behavior will never be forgotten. When readers were asked to stand up three-fourths of them rose. After sitting on the ground for hours they were still eager to listen. They regarded attendance on this anniversary as one of the greatest privileges of their lives. Many said that it seemed as though Christ Himself were speaking to them. Though public exercises filled up most of the two days, several meetings for consultation and prayer were held by the women alone. One was in the interest of the Mite Society, which trains them to intelligent interest in systematic giving for the advancement of the kingdom of Christ in the earth. Another was in the interest of the women's meetings, or Knooshyas as they call them, which meet three times a year, and all on the same day, for the discussion of practical religious subjects relating to personal piety, family life and social duty. For these the whole plain is divided into five districts, and the aim is to hold them in regular order at every large village in each district. The officers are selected from the native women, some of whom have never been even to the seminary, but have been educated by their husbands at home, and yet are among the most capable women in the community. Each meeting is held all day long, with an intermission at noon. Written essays are read on topics previously assigned, and the women discuss the subjects treated of with increasing ability and point. A copy of these papers, which are prepared by Mrs. Shedd, is given to each delegate to read to the women of her own village. The native pastors say that these meetings do much to quicken spiritual life among the women. The afternoon session is a missionary meeting. A monthly letter of missionary information, prepared by Mrs. Dr. Cochran, is sent to the collectors in the various villages to read to all the contributors. In many cases the pastors read them to their congregations. Besides these was a meeting of the graduates of the seminary at sunrise on Wednesday, which was a glad occasion to many who had not met for years, especially those from the mountains. Few could appreciate the intensity of their enjoyment of such privileges. The time was all too short for their reminiscences and earnest words.

In 1885, though the Seminary, through the ill health of the principal, was left mainly in the charge of the native teachers, yet the lessons were carried on with regularity, and six pupils were graduated. There were also several hopeful conversions and an evident growth on the part of professing Christians. In 1886 the interest in spiritual things greatly increased after the week of prayer, and continued to deepen till the end of the year. The older pupils were more conscientious and showed an affectionate interest in the younger scholars. One who had long tried her teachers by her light behavior, confessed with tears that she had been fighting against the Spirit; her convictions were deep and her subsequent apprehension of grace in Christ no less vivid, while her abiding joy and consistent life afterwards was remarked by her companions as well as by her teachers. Nearly the whole school voluntarily attended a daily prayer meeting. In the same spirit they formed societies to labor among the girls of the villages and held meetings like those of the Knooshyas of the women. Essays were read and discussed, and they proved their ability to make the meetings both interesting and profitable.

Mrs. D. P. Cochran has for years been "house mother" in the hospital. Traces of her loving hands appear all through the pleasant, airy wards, in the flowers and pictures; and the clean, comfortable beds, neat curtains and clean floors make all very inviting. The patients appreciate her care and sympathy, and cannot but carry away new ideas of neatness and comfort to their own homes.

Not only are the women organized for church work in some of the larger villages, going from house to house and visiting systematically neighboring hamlets on the Sabbath, but Miss Van Duzee has had a class of from five to fifteen Moslem women, and has taught a young Mûllah, who asked for baptism. She also visited Moslem women at their homes, one of whom took her book with her to the vineyard that her son might teach her to read. As many as two Mohammedan women gave evidence of conversion and remained steadfast under persecution. It is a small beginning, but it is the dawn of a great change in Persia. The Lord hasten it in its time.

Labor among the Nestorians is growing more like labor at home. Instead of national peculiarities, different from ours and therefore conspicuous at first, Christian work moves in a familiar orbit, because it sets out from similar conditions and tends to like results. As the Gospel advances, national traits give place to the spiritual features of the work, common to all lands. The river is most picturesque while yet small high up among the mountains; after it glides into the plain its volume is larger, but its flow is monotonous to the sea. God speed the day when in the placid surface of such a river of life on earth, the Saviour shall see his own likeness reflected, as from the sea of glass above.

INDEX.

Abduction of pupil attempted 58
Abraham Priest 13, 27, 81
Abraham, sister of 55
Accommodation for the night .. 10
Adam and Eve 26
Aintab, Turkey 88
Alpine scenery 29
Amadia 80
Ambassador, visit of 44
Anderson, Rufus D. D 5
Ardeshai, wild women of 26
Asher Khan, persecution by 59
Audible prayer 70
Awakening, an 34

Badal 51, 80
Baxter, Saints Rest 17
Beach, Aaron J 22
Beating of wives 7
Beautiful, Christ become 66
Beds 11
Bethel, the 64
Benevolence of the pupils 88
  "   " " people 89, 90
  "   " " mountains 85, 86
Betrothed, prayer of the 8
Bible as a text book 15
  " blotted with tears 65
  " love for the 15
Births in stables 7
Blood of our necks 61
Boarding school, reasons for ... 13
Boobawa 30, 82
Books, school 15, 16
Bread money 14

Broom, old 65
Buhtan 31
Burials immediately after
  death 49, 52

Care of school 14
Character of women 8
Churdewar 30
Childless mother 62

Christ, self abnegation of 7
Chumba 76
Church organization 92, 93
Closets, behind a quilt 7, 8
  " in manger 66
  " woodroom 34
  " how prized 35, 48, 65
  " marked with tears 75
Clothing of people 6, 14
Coan, Geo. W. Rev 21
Cochran, Deborah W. Mrs 95
Committing to spirit 49
Communion 92
  " farewell 61
Conference, native in mount-
  tains 84
Cost of pupils in seminary 17
Country of Nestorians 6
Crawford, Harriet N 22

Darawe 30
Dark days .... 56—59
Daughters, how regarded 7, 46
Daughter praying 67
Dawood khan 58
Day in seminary 19
Day, Sabbath in seminary 20
Dean, N. Jennie 22
Death bed, first christian 46
Degula, wicked women of 42
Despondency dispelled 43
Dishonesty 10
Divan Khaneh 32
Domestic department in sem-
  inary 18
Dress and diet of pupils 17
Dunkha, Priest 30

Eating to get strength to pray . 69
Education, missionary 16
Eggs in contribution box ... 61, 89
Elias of Buhtan 31
Eneya
Enquirer, first, among the women 24
Eshoo, Priest 37, 46, 48, 53, 57

INDEX.

Esli 21, 64, 85
Excitement, religious 37

Families, situation of 7
Farewell prayer meeting ... 62, 63
Fasts 79
Field, women labor in 7
First fruits .... 46—55
Fiske, Fidelia, early life 5
" arrival of 13
Fiske, Hannah, Mrs. letter to ... 9
Fleas 11
Fuel in the country 7

Gavalan 31
Gawar 28, 82
Geog Tapa 24, 39, 88, 90
Grant, Judith S. Mrs .. 12, 39, 46, 49
Gratitude for spiritual help ... 9, 64
Guly of Seir 80, 82
Guwergis, Deacon ..... 51—55, 58

Half hour, the 19, 20
Hahbie 54
Hammo 31
Hand picking 38, 81
Hanee 13, 22, 62, 66
Hannah of Geog Tapa 50, 51
Hatoon of Geog Tapa 65
Heleneh 8
" of Tiary 73, 76, 77
Hoimar 87, 93
Holladay, Rev. Albert L 12
Home, no word for ...... 6, sec. 11
Home influence, evil ....
.... 13, 17, 38, 39, 74, 75
Hoshebo 22
Hospital 96
Hospitality (Senum's) 11, 55
Houses and housekeeping .. 6, 7, 10
Hymns, Syriac 19

"If you love me lean hard" 25
Ignorance among women 26
Immorality 10, 42
Importunate prayer 60, 61
Isaac, Deacon 56
Ishtazin 28, 83

John, Deacon . 21, 33, 34, 35, 39, 88, 92
Joseph, Deacon 21

Journal of Esli in school 21
Journal of Sarah in the mountains 82
Jubilee 86, 94

Kemat, wife of Werda 79
Keyat 30
Khamis 29, 76
Khanumjan 41
Knooshyas 94
Kûrds 46

Labaree, Benj. Mrs ... 78, 79, 84, 93
Labors for women 24, 38, 42
Labors of pupils 38, 47
Ladies, missionary, unmarried,
  position of 14
Languages studied 16
Letters of Esli 21
  " of Fiske Miss 13, 19
  " of Guly of Seir 80
  " of Joseph Deacon 68
  " of Nazee 77
  " of Rachel 9
  " of Sanum 40
  " of Sarah of Geog Tapa
  .... 81, 82, 83
Letters of Selby of Vizierawa .. 64
  " of Yonam, Deacon 89
Lice 7
Loud prayer 70
Lying 8, 10
Lyon, Mary 71

Manger 11
Marbeeshoo 10
Mardin 31
Mar Elias 12, 91
Mar Ogin 60
Marriages in Persia 41
Marriage of Mar Yohanan 91
Marriage ceremonies 8
Mar Shimon .. 6, 14, 29, 33, 57, 58
Mar Yohanan 12, 31, 32, 58, 91
Mar Yohanan, wife of 90
Massacre of mountaineer 73
Mawana 10
Meetings for women 24, 94
Memikan 28, 30, 82, 92
Mended garments 17
Midnight intercession 43

INDEX.

Mite societies 94
Misky from Bass 79
Monthly concert 67, 71
Monthly concert at Geog Tapa
.... 88, 90
Moressa of Geog Tapa ... 39, 40, 86
Moslem influence 14
Moslem women 12, 96
Mosul 30, 31
Mother, a praying 67
Mother, bereaved 62
Mountain Nestorians ...... 73—87
Mountains, scenery of 29
Mount Holyoke Seminary 16,-
.... 20, 67, 71
Munny 93
Murad Khan 52

Nargis 80
Nazee 73, 76, 77, 78
Nazloo 62, 86
Nazloo river 37
Nerik 83
Nestorians 6
Noisy river 37

Ooreya 29
Oppression 6
Ordination service reformed .. 91
Oshana and Sarah 81, 92
Oxford Seminary, Ohio 20

Passion, outbursts of 8
Patriarch 6
Perkins, Justin, D. D 44
Peril of Seminary 56, 58, 59
Persecution 56, 59, 76
Perseverance in prayer 67, 69
Pins, black 10
Pit, the 50
"Pledge the" 75
Poisoning of Sanun's children . 59
Poverty of people 6, 14
Prayerfulness of Nestorians 60—72
Prayer, behind church in win-
ter 41
Prayer, broken 60
" continuing instant in 69
" importunate 60, 61
" loud 70
" of one 90 years old 40

Prayer on horse back 60
" on roof at midnight 70
" in Degula 68
" in both hemispheres .. 71, 82
" noted week of 68
" meetings 69
" of Esli 64
" specimens of language
in 60, 61, 68
Prayer better than sleep ... 65, 74
Preaching, effects of 33
Profanity 8
Pupils, labors of 38, 47

Quietness produced by the Spirit 21
Quietness in revival of ... 50, 56
Quilt partition 7

Rabi Rachel 86
Rachel (Raheel) 22
Rakhamee and Rukhamee 31
Readers, women, formerly none 8
Repeating a prayer 24
Reports, daily in school ... 18, 19, 20
Resurrection not for women .. 79
Reviling 8
Revivals .... 33—45
" of 1846 .... 34—39
" of 1849 .... 39—42
" of 1850 .... 68—71
" of 1856 .... 43, 44
" of 1857 45
Rhea, Samuel A. Mrs 22
Rice, Mary S. .19, 20, 22, 28, 32, 71, 80
Runaways 13

Saat, women of 30
Sabbath in Seminary 20
Sab. school in Gavalan 32
Sanawar 30
San Francisco 87
Sanum of Gawar .. 34, 40, 46, 59, 62
Sarah of Gawar .... 34, 46—50
Sarah of Tiary 57, 73
Sarah of Geog Tapa 81
Seir 40, 56
Selby of Gavalan 13, 85
Selby of Vizierawa 64
Self denying work for Christ.
.... 86, 88, 90, 91

INDEX

Seminary, attempt at abduction from 16, 22
Seminary, books in 15, 16
Seminary, broken up in 1844 ....
Seminary, daily reports 19
Seminary, day in 19
Seminary, expense 17
Seminary, labors with women in 24
Seminary, Sabbath in 20
Seminary, scholarship of 9, 16
Seminary, teachers in 22
Senum 11
"Settling it" 11
Shedd, I. H. Mrs. 95
Sickness, no provision for 7, sec. 11
Silent devotion 43, 44, 69
Simplicity of converts 37
Sing, too deeply moved to 44
Siyad, Deacon 22, 41
Smoke in houses 6
Speaking in meeting 28
Stealing 8, 10
Stocking, Wm. R. Rev. 26, 27, 28, 32, 34, 47, 54
Stoddard, D. T. Rev. 34, 35, 37, 38, 89
Stoddard, Sophia D. Mrs. 88
Stupidity of women 26

Tamo, Deacon 37, 43
Tears, marks of 75
Tehoma 82

Tent chapel 32
Tergawer 85, 86
Testaments, how paid for 15
Tiary 73, 76
Tiary girls 73

Untidiness 7, 17
Urwintoos 83

Vacation, excursion 31
Vacation, feeling of girls about 38
Van Duzee, Mary K 22, 96
Van Duzee, C. Miss 87
Viragoes 8

Walking concordance 46
Wife learning to pray 66
Will unsubdued 50
Wives beaten 7
Woman, character 8
Woman, position 8
Wright, Austin H. M. D. 13
Wright, J. Mrs 84
Wright, Lucy M 22
Yahya Khan 58
Yakob 35, 92
Yoghoort 11
Yohanan 82
Youan of Geog Tapa 19, 22, 29, 30, 34, 41, 76, 77, 88

Zeer 83

www.ingramcontent.com/pod-product-compliance
Lightning Source LLC
Chambersburg PA
CBHW031123160426
43192CB00008B/1093